MULTICULTURAL MILESTONES IN U.S. HISTORY TO 1900

GLOBE FEARON
Educational Publisher

A Division of Simon & Schuster
Upper Saddle River, New Jersey

On the Cover:

(top left)   John Ross and the Trail of Tears (Chapter 9)

(right)   Mum Bett and the American Slave Trade (Chapter 6)

(bottom left)   Bernardo de Gálvez and the American Revolution (Chapter 5)

Executive Editor: Stephen Lewin
Project Editor: Helene Avraham
Production Director: Penny Gibson
Print Buyers: Cheryl Johnson and Patricia Alvarez
Production Editor: Nicole Cypher
Desktop: Eric Dawson, Margarita T. Linnartz, and José López
Senior Product Manager: Sandra Hutchison
Interior Design: Carole Anson
Cover Design: Eric Dawson
Photo Research: Diana Gongora
Maps: Mapping Specialists
Timelines: Carl Ali Sharif

Photo acknowledgments may be found on page 159.

ISBN 0-835-91115-2

GLOBE FEARON EDUCATIONAL PUBLISHER
A Division of Simon & Schuster
Upper Saddle River, New Jersey

CONTENTS

Maps, Charts, and Graphs

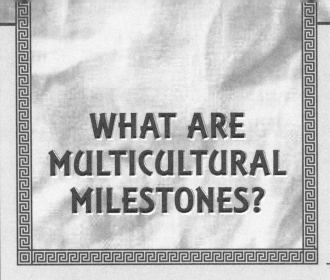

WHAT ARE MULTICULTURAL MILESTONES?

- Who was Mum Bett? How did her struggle help limit slavery?
- Why did the Latino soldier, Bernardo de Gálvez, help the American colonists win the Revolution?
- Why did Clara Barton brave enemy fire and the scorn of male officers to save lives on Civil War battlefields?
- How did Luis Muñoz Rivera fight for the integrity of Puerto Ricans after the United States took over this island?

Don't rush to your American history textbook for answers to these questions. The information should be there, but it isn't. Americans such as Barton, Bett, Gálvez, and Rivera helped shape the United States. But these people are just a few of the many Americans whose story remains untold despite their contributions to American history. It is the purpose of the book you are reading, *Multicultural Milestones in United States History*, to shine a light on some great Americans whose history has been buried in obscurity.

HISTORY "WRITTEN BY THE WINNERS"

Why don't we know more about these Americans? The answer lies in a famous saying: *History was written by the victor.* In other words, the history of our country was mainly written by people who came from the groups which dominated our country. In deciding what to write about, they chose events that made their groups look good.

For many years, our historians came from the culture that controlled our society and government. For the most part, these people were white and male. Most of their roots were in northern and western Europe. They worked hard, believed in the dream of American liberty, and contributed much to our heritage. However, they often failed to see the contributions of people from other backgrounds.

The traditional histories tell of the democratic ideals of equality and justice. However, they do not tell enough about how these ideals were not practiced. The histories also did not tell of the achievements of people from other cultures. The traditional histories were honest. But they did not tell the full story.

HISTORY FROM A MULTICULTURAL PERSPECTIVE

Many of the historians of the past came from one culture. Yet, the United States does not have a single culture. It is **multicultural,** or a nation of many cultures. In fact, the United States is probably the most diverse nation on earth. Americans have their roots in every country of the world. They have brought many different customs and traditions with them. They have contributed to our history in ways that were not mentioned by traditional historians.

Slaves preparing cotton; Chapter 14

German immigrants; Chapter 8

Elementary school woodcut, 1866; Chapter 7

James Armistead, born 1748; Chapter 6

Reception of Cortéz by Montezuma; Chapter 1

Multicultural Milestones in United States History tells the stories of some of the people and events that shaped our history. Their stories have been left out of U.S. history books for too long. If this book helps awaken an appreciation of that story, it will have accomplished its mission.

Multicultural Milestones in United States History is not meant to replace your textbook. Rather, it is meant to supplement it. The stories in these chapters will enrich your study of American history by providing another perspective on the events you study.

WHAT AMERICANS SHARE

Multicultural Milestones in United States History celebrates the accomplishments of different Americans. Americans differ in some ways from one another, but are alike in as many ways as they are different.

1. Americans share many ideals. Many of them were written in our Declaration of Independence and Constitution. We believe in **democracy.** Democracy is a form of government in which citizens rule, either directly or indirectly, through elected representatives.

2. Americans believe in the right to live happy and healthy lives.

3. We believe that citizens and the government should respect the rights of all the people.

4. Finally, Americans share a common future. We believe that the United States is a place where people can improve their lives.

STRENGTH IN DIVERSITY

When the United States became a new nation in 1776, it was already diverse. Many Americans had their roots in West Africa and Northern and Western Europe. Native Americans practiced many different cultures. In the 1800s, many Latinos became citizens of the United States. From 1820 to 1990, about 59 million people immigrated to the United States. These people came from all over the world.

The mixing of people has had a major impact on U.S. history. Many times, people did not mix happily. We have seen examples of deadly conflict between Americans. We have seen that Americans sometimes discriminated against each other. However, diversity has also made the United States great. Despite conflict, we are stronger because we are diverse.

Luis Muñoz Rivera; Chapter 16

Queen Liliuokalani; Chapter 15

Chinese farm workers; Chapter 11

Civil War nurses; Chapter 12

Civil War soldiers; Chapter 13

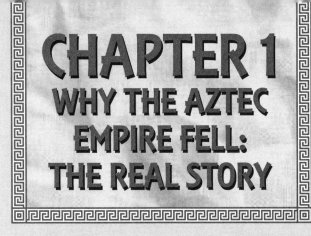

CHAPTER 1
WHY THE AZTEC EMPIRE FELL: THE REAL STORY

The emperor, Montezuma, greeted the Spanish warmly, little knowing that the more gold he gave them, the more they wanted it all.

PEOPLE, PLACES, AND EVENTS

Hernán Cortés
Tenochtitlán
Montezuma
Cuauhtémoc

VOCABULARY

tribute
causeway

MULTICULTURAL MILESTONES

- The Aztec rose up against Cortés's forces and drove them from the capital.
- Smallpox and other diseases brought by the Europeans devastated the Aztec.
- The Aztec were conquered by the Spanish.

PATHS TO THE PRESENT: CHANGING VIEWS

A famous person dies, someone whom you have always admired. The media has celebrated this person, made him or her seem very glamorous. Then it turns out that this person was not the angel that he or she seemed. Rather than glamorous, happy, and generous, the person was angry, brutal, and selfish. You are shocked.

In the same way that our view of a person may change, our view of historical events may change. Take the case of the Aztecs. We know that the Aztec empire fell after the invasion of Hernán Cortés (kohr-TES). Earlier histories praised the bravery and faith of the Spanish conquerors. But was it Cortés and his few Spanish soldiers who defeated the Aztec or was it something else? This chapter describes what really led to the fall of the Aztec empire.

SETTING THE STAGE: A SEARCH FOR WEALTH

When the first Spanish explorers reached the Americas, the empire of the Aztec was powerful, but not old. The Aztec had come into the Valley of Mexico around the year A.D. 1250.

In the early 1400s, the Aztec began to expand. They conquered one city after another. By 1519, the emperor Montezuma (mahn-tuh-ZYOO-muh) ruled a land of 35 provinces. In it were as many as 30 million people, far more than in any nation of Europe at that time.

Wealth poured into the capital city of Tenochtitlán (teh-nohch-tee-TLAHN). All conquered peoples had to pay **tribute,** a kind of tax in goods or services, to the Aztec. Defeated cities sent gold, jewels, animal skins, slaves, food, and much, much more.

In 1519, it seemed that Aztec power was overwhelming. Montezuma commanded an army of up to 200,000. They had carried Aztec rule from the Caribbean to the Pacific.

Then the Spanish arrived. The Spanish who invaded Mexico were led by Hernán Cortés. He assembled 11 ships and convinced some 750 people—Spaniards, Africans, and Native Americans from the Caribbean islands—to join him. In Mexico, the Spanish found wealth beyond their wildest dreams. That wealth helped build a Spanish empire in the Americas that lasted for more than 300 years. Stories of the wealth would lead other European nations to start settlements in the Americas.

The question has long been asked: how did such a small band of Spanish manage to defeat the mighty Aztec? In the past, historians answered that the bravery and faith of the Spanish were responsible. Today, we know that more was behind the fall of the Aztec.

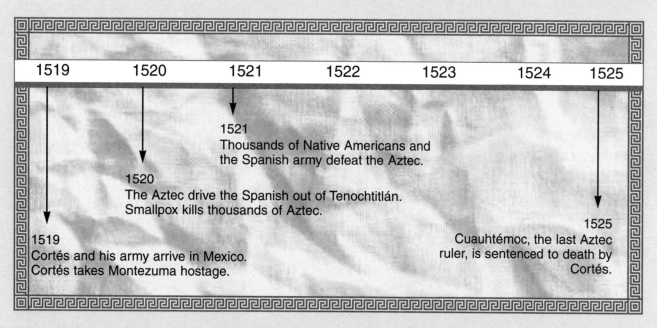

| 1519 | 1520 | 1521 | 1522 | 1523 | 1524 | 1525 |

1521
Thousands of Native Americans and the Spanish army defeat the Aztec.

1520
The Aztec drive the Spanish out of Tenochtitlán. Smallpox kills thousands of Aztec.

1519
Cortés and his army arrive in Mexico. Cortés takes Montezuma hostage.

1525
Cuauhtémoc, the last Aztec ruler, is sentenced to death by Cortés.

In November 1519, about 400 Spaniards marched across the **causeway,** a raised road over the lake that led to the Aztec capital Tenochtitlán. It seemed that almost all of the city's 250,000 residents had come to watch the arrival of the strangers. One Spaniard described the crowd:

> The numbers were too great to count the men, women, and boys in the streets, on the rooftops and in canoes on the waterways, who had come out to see us.

The Aztec ruler Montezuma was there to greet the strangers. He led the 200 richly dressed nobles who met the strangers at the entrance to the city. Montezuma welcomed Cortés warmly, offering him a splendid gold necklace. Montezuma thought that these strangers might be gods and did not wish to offend them.

Montezuma treated his Spanish guests well. He settled them in a huge palace. He led them on tours of the city. The Spanish saw the marketplace, the temples, and the zoo.

Cortés and his soldiers were impressed with the city. They made plans to capture Tenochtitlán for Spain. Realizing that they were greatly outnumbered, they thought of a plan. The Spanish seized Montezuma and held him hostage. They believed that as long as they held him they were safe.

SECTION 1:
THE AZTEC WIN THE FIRST ROUND.

With Montezuma hostage, the Spanish grew bolder. They raided the Aztec treasury. One Aztec writer says, "They rushed in everywhere, each one stealing for himself. They were totally possessed by greed." Taking Aztec gold, however, was just the beginning.

By rallying the support of Native Americans, Cortés was finally able to defeat the Aztec.

Fighting Back In May, the Aztec celebrated a holy day at Tenochtitlán. As nobles sang and danced, Spanish soldiers with drawn swords rushed in. The Spanish massacred over 200 Aztec leaders.

The Aztec people stormed the palace, trying to get at the Spanish. Spanish cannons and crossbows stopped the attack. But, the Spanish were trapped. They were prisoners in Montezuma's palace.

Cortés took Montezuma to the roof of the palace. He thought the ruler might convince the Aztec to stop the attack.

From the walls of the palace, the Spanish could see the city stretching out before them. The plaza in front of the palace was filled with angry Aztec.

A young noble named Cuauhtémoc (kwow-TEH-mohk) led the group. Cuauhtémoc was the cousin of the Aztec ruler. Aztec anger now turned on Montezuma. The Aztec blamed him for letting the Spanish into the city.

Montezuma spoke, trying to calm the Aztec. Cuauhtémoc cut him off quickly.

> We do not believe your words any more, Montezuma. We will not obey you because you are no longer our

king. You stopped being our king when you gave in to the Spanish. You deserve whatever punishment is given to a wicked man.

The Aztec began throwing rocks and stones at the ruler. One story says Montezuma died from a stone flung by Cuauhtémoc. Another story says the Spanish killed him.

Retreat from Tenochtitlán With Montezuma's death, things looked bad for the Spanish. Their hostage was dead. Food and water were running low. They had to break out from the city if they hoped to live.

Cortés had learned that the Aztec were not used to fighting at night. So, after midnight in the darkness of June 30, 1520, he led his troops out of the palace. Moving as quietly as possible, they reached one of the causeways. Escape was in sight when an Aztec woman raised the alarm.

The Aztec generals had organized their troops well. In moments, thousands of Aztec swinging clubs and swords charged the Spanish.

The Spanish slashed and hacked at their attackers and stumbled toward the end of the causeway. Cortés made it to safety, then turned back to help others. But almost 600 Spaniards died on what came to be called *la noche triste*, "the Night of Sorrows."

The surviving Spanish fled from the Valley of Mexico. The Aztec chased them for a while, but then returned home. They thought the strangers were gone for good.

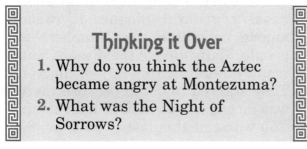

Thinking it Over
1. Why do you think the Aztec became angry at Montezuma?
2. What was the Night of Sorrows?

Aztec arms were no match for the well armed Spanish. Here two warriors face each other.

SECTION 2:
THE AZTEC EMPIRE ENDS.

In July 1520, the Aztec thought they were safe. Cortés's forces seemed shattered. He had lost almost half his soldiers. Tenochtitlán seemed as strong as ever. Chances of the Spanish conquering it seemed small.

Yet little over a year later, Tenochtitlán and the Aztec empire were in ruins. The Spanish held Montezuma's former lands. How had this happened?

Spanish Advantages   In the year between the Night of Sorrows and their final victory, the Spanish got help from different sources. First, ships arrived with more Spanish soldiers.

The Spanish also brought more cannons and muskets. Muskets were old-time guns that could kill at great distances. Cannons could cut down groups of Aztec warriors or batter down walls.

The Spanish also used their skill in shipbuilding. They cut wood and laid out 13 small ships. When the ships were done, they were carried over the mountains in pieces to the lake in which Tenochtitlán sat. The ships were put together and armed with cannons. Now the Spanish could attack the Aztec city from the lake as well as from the causeways.

The Spanish also fought differently than the Aztec did. Each Aztec fought as an individual, seeking to win honor and glory. The Aztec fought, not to kill their enemies, but to capture them. They wanted captives to sacrifice to their gods.

The Spanish, on the other hand, fought as a unit. They could advance and retreat, wheel and turn on signal. Also, they fought to kill their enemies, not take them alive.

Aztec Enemies   Still, Spanish weapons and styles of fighting were not the main reasons the Spanish won. Cortés had other help.

Soon after landing in Mexico, he learned that many of the peoples the Aztec had conquered hated the Aztec. They resented paying tribute. They felt deep anger at seeing their young men and women sacrificed to Aztec gods.

Cortés played on this anger toward the Aztec. He offered aid to people defeated by the Aztec. He promised to help free them from Aztec rule. Hatred of the Aztec was so strong that he soon won many allies.

When Cortés first marched into Tenochtitlán in 1519, thousands of soldiers from the city of Tlaxcala (tlash-KA-lah) marched with him. That city had been the most bitter foe of Tenochtitlán.

Other cities joined the Spanish. The Spaniards were their strongest hope of ending Aztec rule. They thought that once the Aztec were defeated, the Spaniards would go home. They had no way of knowing that the Spaniards planned to stay and rule in the Americas. By the summer of 1521, Cortés commanded an army of almost 100,000 Native American fighters.

The Power of Disease   The most powerful ally the Spanish had was disease. The Spanish carried to the Americas diseases that had long been common in Europe. Among them were measles, mumps, whooping cough, and chickenpox. Those diseases were often deadly in Europe then. But Europeans usually caught them as children. People who survived became immune to, or able to resist, further attacks. Such diseases were unknown in the Americas. No one was immune to them. They would be deadly.

A Spanish soldier who marched with Cortés in 1520 carried one of these European diseases, smallpox. Unknowingly, he passed it on to Native Americans in Mexico. An Aztec account tells what happened after the Spaniards had left Tenochtitlán on the Night of Sorrows.

> There came among us a great sickness, a general plague. It raged among us, killing vast numbers of people. Many died of the disease, and many others died merely of hunger. They starved to death because there was no one left alive to care for them. The worst of this lasted 60 days, 60

days of horror. And when this had happened, the Spaniards returned.

Almost half of the Aztec who caught the disease died. The disease killed nobles and slaves, soldiers and farmers, adults and children. The Aztec government and army were badly weakened. The whole nation was in confusion.

Wiped Out Europeans would spread these diseases throughout the Americas. Everywhere, the diseases would devastate the Native Americans. In the 1520s, European diseases reached Peru. Disease shook the Inca empire there and cleared the way for Spanish conquest.

Similar events took place in North America, too. Shortly before the English Pilgrims landed in New England in 1620, disease had raced through the forests killing Native Americans there. As a result, there were few Native Americans left to resist the building of an English colony in what would become Massachusetts.

The Last Battle An Aztec noble ruled briefly after the death of Montezuma. But he died of smallpox soon after the *noche triste*. Cuauhtémoc survived. The 22-year-old became the last Aztec ruler. He tried to rally his people to defeat the Spanish.

> Remember the bold hearts of our ancestors who, though few in number, dared to enter this land and conquer it. Do not be cowardly. Do not scorn [reject] me because of my youth.

Cuauhtémoc asked nearby cities for help. One ruler replied: "How would I gain by sending men to you, for we are always at war. Let the strangers kill the Aztec."

Cuauhtémoc then prepared for the final attack. He gathered weapons.

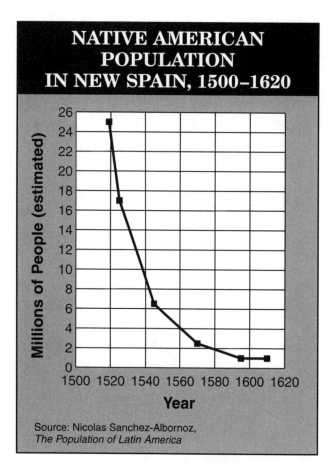

NATIVE AMERICAN POPULATION IN NEW SPAIN, 1500–1620

Source: Nicolas Sanchez-Albornoz, *The Population of Latin America*

What does the chart show about Native American population? What is the reason for the change?

He strengthened the city's walls and built barricades in its streets. He waited.

In May 1521, the Spanish attack began. The 900 Spanish and their 100,000 Native American allies took control of the causeways. The Spanish ships drove Aztec canoes off the lake. Soon, Tenochtitlán was sealed off. No food or supplies could enter.

Still, the Aztec fought on. The Spanish had to take the city house by house. Buildings were torn down or burned. Aztec taken prisoner were slaughtered. Cortés urged Cuauhtémoc to surrender, but he refused. For 93 days the Aztec resisted.

Finally, on August 13, 1521, the battle was over. There was no longer a city to fight for. Tenochtitlán lay in ruins. An Aztec poet described the scene:

> In the roads lie the broken spears.
> Without roofs are the houses,
> And red are their walls with blood.
> The waters have turned crimson [red], as if they were dyed,
> And when we drink them they are salty with blood.

The Last Aztec Ruler Cuauhtémoc survived the battle. He was taken prisoner and brought to Cortés. The Aztec prisoner then spoke to his conqueror:

> I have done everything in my power to defend myself and my people, and everything that it was my duty to do. You may do with me whatever you wish, so kill me, for that will be best.

Cortés did not kill Cuauhtémoc then. The Aztec king was too valuable. The Spanish kept Cuauhtémoc as a prisoner. They tortured him, hoping to find more Aztec gold. They found little, but they left him disabled.

Cortés used Cuauhtémoc in other ways. He had the king organize the Aztec to begin clearing the rubble that had once been Tenochtitlán. There, Native American workers began to build a Spanish city.

Cortés never let Cuauhtémoc get far from him. He feared that if the noble escaped he might lead an uprising of the Aztec. In 1525, Cortés led an expedition south to what is now Honduras. On the way, Cortés charged that Cuauhtémoc had tried to start a rebellion. Far from his home, Cuauhtémoc was hanged by the Spanish.

Their city in ruins, the Aztec were forced to destroy their hallowed religious shrines.

Cuauhtémoc's courage and resistance made him a hero to Mexico's people. Today, a statue of him rises in Mexico City, not far from where his palace once stood. It is a fitting monument to the last Aztec ruler, whose name can be translated as "Fallen Eagle" or "Setting Sun."

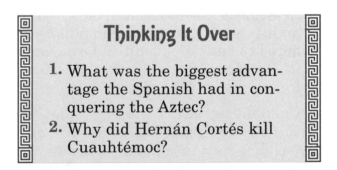

Thinking It Over

1. What was the biggest advantage the Spanish had in conquering the Aztec?
2. Why did Hernán Cortés kill Cuauhtémoc?

CHAPTER 1 REVIEW

I. REVIEWING VOCABULARY

Match each word on the left with the correct definition on the right.

1. Tenochtitlán
2. tribute
3. causeway

a. a tax conquered people pay to conquerors
b. the capital city of the Aztec
c. a raised road over a body of water

II. UNDERSTANDING THE CHAPTER

1. Who was the ruler of the Aztec at the time of the Spanish arrival?
2. How did the Spanish soldiers in the Aztec capital try to ensure their safety?
3. How did smallpox affect the ability of the Aztec to resist the Spanish?
4. Why did other Native Americans aid Cortés against the Aztec?

III. APPLYING YOUR SKILLS

1. **Comparing** (a) What types of weapons and tactics did Spanish and Aztec soldiers use? (b) Which side had the more effective weapons and tactics? Explain.
2. **Analyzing a Quotation** Read the following statement made by Cuauhtémoc *"Our enemies used to be Tlaxcala and Cholula, but now we must also face Texcoco, Chalco, Xochimilco and even Tacuba."* What problem facing the Aztec is he speaking about?

IV. WRITING ABOUT HISTORY

1. **What Would You Have Done?** You are a Mexican patriot dedicating the statue of Cuauhtémoc described on page 16. Write an inscription for the base of the statue that describes Cuauhtémoc's place in Mexican history.
2. **Past to Present** Read again the quotation from the speech made by Cuauhtémoc on page 15. Then write a short speech intended to convince a group of older people that you are capable of leading a campaign to improve your neighborhood in some way.

V. WORKING TOGETHER

1. Meet in small groups. Each group should create a panel for an illustrated storyboard showing the major events in the Spanish conquest of the Aztec.
2. Divide into small groups. Using information from your school or local library, draw posters that show what typical Spanish and Aztec soldiers of the early 1500s looked like, what clothing and armor they wore, and what weapons they carried.

CHAPTER 2
FROM AFRICAN PRINCE TO AMERICAN SLAVE

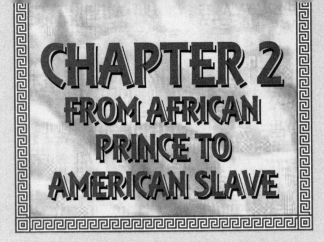

Brought as servants, Africans in Virginia were soon made slaves. As slaves, they faced appalling work conditions in tobacco fields.

PEOPLE, PLACES, AND EVENTS

Timbuktu
American Colonization Society
Liberia

VOCABULARY

Koran
cavalry
ransom
slave codes

MULTICULTURAL MILESTONES

- The first African servants in the Americas were able to earn freedom.
- Africans were forced into life-long enslavement in the Americas.
- Abd al-Rahman Ibrahima and his wife returned to Africa.

PATHS TO THE PRESENT: RICHES TO RAGS

How would you like to be born rich? You have everything you want. You are educated in the best universities. You are a born leader and a great warrior. Sounds great, doesn't it?

But then something horrible happens. You lose everything. For the rest of your life, you live as a slave in a strange land. You are forced to do the hardest work and have all your freedoms taken away. This is not a piece of fiction, or a made up story. This is exactly what happened to al-Rahman Ibrahima. He was born a prince. Then, through a series of events, he became a slave. How Ibrahima coped with this disaster can help us understand how Africans found the strength to withstand slavery.

SETTING THE STAGE: THE JOURNEY INTO SLAVERY

In 1619, 20 African captives were brought to Jamestown, Virginia. The first Africans in Virginia were servants rather than slaves. They had the same rights as those of white servants. Once they finished the terms of their contract, they became free. Some even prospered. One such person was Anthony Johnson.

Anthony Johnson arrived in Jamestown in 1621 as an indentured servant. A year later he gained his freedom. By 1651, he was rich enough to import five servants of his own. For this, the Virginia government granted him 250 acres of land. Some of his servants were Africans, but others were European.

In the first 40 years of English rule, Africans could acquire land. They could also vote and testify in court. Race did not seem to be a problem. Africans and whites worked together in the fields.

Gradually, however, the differences between white and African servants grew sharper. Those colonies that used African labor began to pass laws saying that Africans had to remain servants for as long as they lived. Even the children of African laborers would have to serve forever. In other words, they were slaves.

Some historians suggest as many as 20 million Africans were forced to make the journey to America as slaves. Others put the number at 14 million. How many died we will also never know. Ibrahima's story is unusual for a number of reasons. First, he wrote about his experiences. Second, he was able to return to Africa. Millions of other captives never saw their homeland again.

1600	1650	1700	1750	1800	1850

1787
Fula prince Abd al-Rahman Ibrahima is captured in battle and sold into slavery in the United States.

1651
African American Anthony Johnston is granted land in Virginia.

1829
Ibrahima wins his freedom and returns to Africa. He dies in Liberia.

1816
Ibrahima writes a letter to his family in Africa.

1619
The first Africans are brought to North America as servants.

1817
The American Colonization Society sets up the colony of Liberia in West Africa

The forced movement of Africans to the Americas lasted nearly 400 years! Millions of Africans were taken to the Americas. They provided labor that made their owners wealthy and made the lands very productive. But the price paid by the Africans who were enslaved was very high. The story of Abd al-Rahman Ibrahima helps us understand who these Africans were. It shows us the horror they felt to be enslaved, what effects slavery had on them, and how they fought to preserve their way of life.

SECTION 1:
A PRINCE BECOMES ENSLAVED.

Abd al-Rahman Ibrahima was born in 1762 in a farming region of the present country of Guinea (GIN-ee). It is a beautiful area of green mountains and grassy plains.

Ibrahima was a member of the powerful Fula people. As a son of one of the nine chieftains, he was expected to become a leader of his people when he became an adult.

When Ibrahima was twelve, he was sent to Timbuktu to study. Timbuktu was a center of learning and one of the largest cities in West Africa. The city attracted scholars from Africa, Europe and Asia. Medicine, mathematics, law, and religion were taught. The religion of Islam had swept across Africa from the Middle East and young Ibrahima was raised in the Muslim tradition.

A Leader of His People When he returned home, Ibrahima could read and write Arabic. He knew the **Koran,** the Muslim holy book, very well. Ibrahima married and became the father of several children. In his mid-twenties, he became a leader of the Fula **cavalry** in their war

Timbuktu, capital of the Mali empire, was a city of handsome new buildings, great wealth, and some of the world's finest universities.

with the neighboring Mandingo people. A cavalry is a group of soldiers that fight on horseback.

The battle seemed to be going well. Ibrahima's horse soldiers attacked with spears, bows, slings, and swords. The enemy retreated into the forested mountains. Ibrahima's men chased them, but soon found they had stepped into a trap. Ibrahima heard rifles firing and men about him falling dead. The firing was coming from both sides. The courage of the Fula was no match for the Mandingo guns. Ibrahima was hit in the back by an arrow. Then something smashed against his head and knocked him out.

When he came to, he tried to move his arms, but they were tied with a heavy rope. He was now a prisoner. The victorious Mandingos stripped him of his clothes and sandals. They pushed him roughly into file with the other captives. They then began a long trip that would eventually take them to the sea.

Permanent Slavery It was common practice among warring African people that prisoners taken in battle were held for long periods. Sometimes they could be used as hostages against future attack. Sometimes they were sent back to their original people in exchange for goods. Chiefs who were captured were often **ransomed,** or returned in exchange for money or other prisoners.

Ibrahima knew that this time things were different. The journey to the sea took weeks. All the captives were tied to each other with ropes around their necks. They walked from sun up to sun down. Those who could not keep up were sometimes speared and left to die. When they reached the sea, they were inspected, then put into irons. They were loaded onto a small boat that took them out to a much larger ship.

The ship was already crowded with African captives. The white men on the ship looked very strange to the captured Africans. Many of the Africans had never seen a white man before. The whites had long hair, red faces, and spoke a language the Africans had never heard before. Ibrahima and the others were shoved toward an open hatch.

Voyage of Horror They were forced "between decks." This was the area below the main deck and above the cargo hold. The area was like a shelf, usually about five feet high. From the sides of the ship, rough wooden planks extended six to nine feet toward the center. Here the captives lived. There were no mattresses, sheets, pillows, or blankets. There was only hard wood.

A typical slave ship had two or three such shelves. These held as many as 700 people. The space between the shelves was often less than three feet. The captives were bound in pairs by the ankles and wrists.

Joined together by chains neck to neck, captured African villagers are marched through forests, and along rivers to the African coast. Those who fell ill were left to die. At the coast, they were loaded on ships bound for the Americas. Their suffering had just begun.

The area was dark and the smell overpowering. Each shelf had two or three buckets for use as toilets. But in the darkness, the buckets were often spilled or knocked over. Not being used to traveling on a ship, many captives became sick and vomited on themselves. If they refused to eat the strange foods the white men offered, they were beaten.

The place where Ibrahima and the other captives were put was very hot. There they lay all day, gasping for air. Their muscles cramped. Iron cut into their legs and wrists. People were so crowded between decks that there was often no room even to turn around in. Soon many were ill. In these close quarters, many died. Some slave ships lost half of their human cargo during the journey. The death rate averaged between 13 and 20 percent.

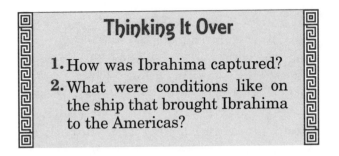

Thinking It Over

1. How was Ibrahima captured?
2. What were conditions like on the ship that brought Ibrahima to the Americas?

SECTION 2:
IBRAHIMA RETURNS TO AFRICA.

As Ibrahima's ship approached land, the Africans were finally brought onto the deck. They were fed. Sailors put oil on the skins of some of the Africans so that they would look better. The sores that had developed where their irons had rubbed the skin raw were treated. To cover their sores, the Africans were given clothes to wear.

No other part of slavery was dreaded more by African American slaves than the possibility of being sold and separated from families. Such a possibility is becoming real to this family shown being sold at an auction in 1819.

FROM AFRICAN PRINCE TO AMERICAN SLAVE

The ship had landed in Mississippi. Ibrahima and the others were led off the ship. Even though he understood no English, he knew that the white men who stood around him were bargaining for him. He was told to turn around and several of the white men near him examined his teeth, looked into his eyes, and made him move around to be sure he was not lame.

Eventually he was bought by Thomas Foster. Foster was a tobacco grower. Ibrahima was his third slave. Foster agreed to pay $930 for Ibrahima and a young boy who came on the same ship.

The Will to Survive The "breaking in" period for newly arrived slaves such as Ibrahima was likely to be harsh. Slaves were often beaten. Because their resistance was low from the difficult journey, many became sick.

Ibrahima tried to explain that he was the son of a king. He offered a ransom for his release, but no one would listen. Foster probably had never heard of the Fula or of their culture. In his mind, he had paid good money for the African and wasn't going to give him up.

Ibrahima was confused and depressed. Just a few months ago, he had been an educated man and leader of his people. Now he was a prisoner in a strange land where the language and customs were unlike those of his own country. He was very depressed at the thought that he might never see his family again.

Like most slaves, Ibrahima was ordered to work in the fields. He refused. In his native country, he and his people were shepherds. They knew little about farm work.

Ibrahima was whipped until he passed out. The pain was terrible, but the pain he felt within was even greater. He lost all hope. He agreed to work in the fields.

His work day lasted from day break until late in the evening. After a few months of this, Ibrahima could see no end in sight. He decided to escape.

Native Americans and Slavery Before Africans were taken captive and shipped to the American colonies, the white farmers had attempted to enslave Native Americans. But Native Americans often died from the white man's diseases or from the very hard work. Many escaped to the woods which they knew better than their captors.

Africans were imported to take the place of the Native Americans. The enslaved Africans were thousands of miles from their friends and family. Furthermore, their skin color made them instantly recognizable. Escape seemed almost impossible.

Escape One night, Ibrahima ran away from the Foster plantation. For a while he lived in the forest eating wild berries and fruit. He believed he couldn't trust anyone, white or black. Sometimes he saw men with dogs and knew they were searching for runaways. Maybe they were looking for him.

He grew more and more desperate. Ibrahima did not know the country. He did not know how far he was from his homeland or how to get back. He knew that this place was ruled by white men with guns. The other Africans Ibrahima had seen were from all parts of Africa. Even if they could speak his language, they were afraid because it was forbidden to speak African languages around the whites. Ibrahima had two choices. He could stay in the woods and probably die, or he could return to slavery.

Ibrahima decided to return to the Foster plantation. He was whipped and when he recovered from his wounds, he returned to work.

Ibrahima was enslaved not only by Foster, but by the society in which he now lived. Enslaved people were governed by what was known as **slave codes.** Slave travel was limited. Enslaved people could not meet in groups without a white person present. Slaves found guilty of serious crimes, such as striking a white person, were hanged. In some places it was forbidden to teach slaves to read or write.

A Chance Meeting By 1807, Ibrahima had been enslaved for 20 years. He had remarried and had a new family. At age 45, he was no longer as useful to Foster. Foster did not worry that Ibrahima would run away again. So he gave Ibrahima a few rights that other slaves did not have. Ibrahima was allowed to grow a few vegetables on his own and sell them in town. It was in town one day that he met Andrew Marschalk.

Marschalk was fascinated by Ibrahima's story. He urged him to write a letter to his people telling them of his whereabouts. Maybe they would buy his freedom.

Ibrahima had lost almost all hope, so for a long time he did nothing. Finally in 1816, Ibrahima wrote the letter that Marschalk suggested. Marschalk had little knowledge of Africa so he sent the letter not to Guinea, but to another African country, Morocco.

The government of Morocco did not know Ibrahima. But the letter was written in Arabic and made it clear that Ibrahima was a Muslim. Moroccan officials appealed to U.S. President James Monroe to free Ibrahima. The letter landed on the desk of the American Secretary of State, Henry Clay. Clay wrote to Foster about Ibrahima and asked for his release.

Back to Africa Foster was angry and refused to free Ibrahima. But after many letters and pressure from the State Department, Foster gave in. He agreed to release Ibrahima if the African promised to leave the country and return to his homeland.

Without money, Ibrahima had little hope of returning to Africa. Fortunately, a group of Virginians had founded an organization to return to Africa, African Americans who had been freed from slavery. This group was called the American Colonization Society. In 1817, they bought land in West Africa and started a colony called Liberia.

By now Ibrahima's story was well known. Many people worked to win his freedom and that of his wife. On February 7, 1829, Ibrahima and his wife set sail for Africa. After years of slavery, he was a free man about to go home. Sadly, he died in July, 1829 in Liberia without ever seeing his Fula homeland again.

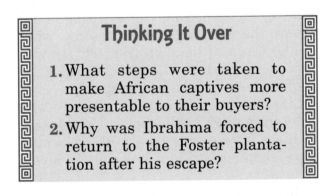

Thinking It Over

1. What steps were taken to make African captives more presentable to their buyers?
2. Why was Ibrahima forced to return to the Foster plantation after his escape?

CHAPTER 2 REVIEW

I. REVIEWING VOCABULARY

Match each word on the left with the correct definition on the right.

1. cavalry
2. ransom
3. slave codes

    a. laws that took rights away from enslaved people
    b. payment to free prisoners
    c. groups of soldiers who fight on horseback

II. UNDERSTANDING THE CHAPTER

1. In what city did young Ibrahima study?
2. Why was Ibrahima depressed when he reached the Foster plantation?
3. Why did the attempt to enslave Native Americans fail?
4. To what African country did Ibrahima return?

III. APPLYING YOUR SKILLS

1. **Drawing Conclusions** A conclusion is a statement supported by facts. Read the following statement. Then list any facts that you can find in the chapter to support it: "One of the reasons why slavery took hold in the United States was because the work was so grueling that free persons would not do it."

2. **Evaluating** Some groups that have been treated unfairly have received compensation for mistreatment. For example, Japanese Americans who were interned during World War II received compensation because their rights were violated. Do you think the descendants of Africans brought to the United States against their will should also be compensated to make up for mistreatment under slavery? Explain why or why not.

IV. WRITING ABOUT HISTORY

1. **What Would You Have Done?** You are Ibrahima after your failed escape attempt. Write a letter to your family in Africa explaining how you feel, why you decided to escape, and why you returned.

2. **Past to Present** Write a play that compares Ibrahima's life with someone else who has struggled with a major tragedy. Scenes from Ibrahima's life might include his early life, capture, life under slavery, and return to Africa.

V. WORKING TOGETHER

Working in small groups, prepare bulletin board displays about Ibrahima's life. Include a map that shows Fula land in present-day Guinea, the Mississippi River delta where the Foster plantation was, and Liberia. The display might also include drawings showing traditional African villages, Timbuktu, and slave ships.

CHAPTER 3
THE COMANCHE AND THE SPANISH STRUGGLE FOR THE PLAINS

PEOPLE, PLACES, AND EVENTS

Apache
Comanche
San Sabá
Battle of Red River

VOCABULARY

mission
missionary
presidio
nomad

MULTICULTURAL MILESTONES

- The Spanish begin to establish settlements in Texas.
- The Comanche attack the Spanish mission at San Sabá.

A cowhide painting from the early 1700s, shows mounted Native Americans allied with the Spanish attacking an Apache village.

PATHS TO THE PRESENT: THIS IS MY LAND!

Our histories tell us that after the Europeans arrived in the Americas, they established permanent settlements. As these settlements grew, Europeans came into conflict with Native Americans who inhabited the lands. It seemed as if wherever Europeans settled, they pushed Native Americans from their traditional lands.

Actually, the Europeans were not always successful in taking over land. We know that the first British settlements in North America nearly failed in their early years.

In Texas, Native American groups kept the Spanish out for over one hundred years. Indeed, in the end, the Comanche defeated the Spanish and drove them from Texas. This story, which is not in traditional history books, is the subject of this chapter.

SETTING THE STAGE: SPAIN'S AMERICAN EMPIRE

By the 1600s, Spain had a mighty empire in the Americas. It controlled most of Mexico and Central America. Spain also held large parts of South America.

Spain now tried to expand north from Mexico. One reason was competition from other European nations. By the late 1600s, both England and France had settlements in North America. Spanish officials saw France as the main threat. The Spanish feared that a French settlement on the Texas coast would be used to raid Spanish ships in the Gulf of Mexico.

The best way to stop the French from moving into Texas was to build Spanish forts there. In 1690, the Spanish built some small settlements in East Texas. Those settlements did not last long because of disease. In 1693, the settlements were abandoned. However, new reports of French settlements changed the minds of the Spanish. Spain returned to Texas in the 1720s. Within a few years, the Spanish had built a chain of **missions** across Texas. A mission is a settlement whose chief purpose is to convert people to the Christian religion.

Spanish settlers never came to Texas in large numbers. Texas was a long journey from Mexico across a harsh, rugged land. Mexico had bustling cities, rich silver mines, and large estates with plenty of Native American workers. Texas seemed to offer only hard work and the threat of raids by Native Americans.

One of the few settlements that did take root was near San Antonio. The missions near San Antonio had the most Native Americans of any in Texas. This gave Spanish officials hope of expanding control over Texas.

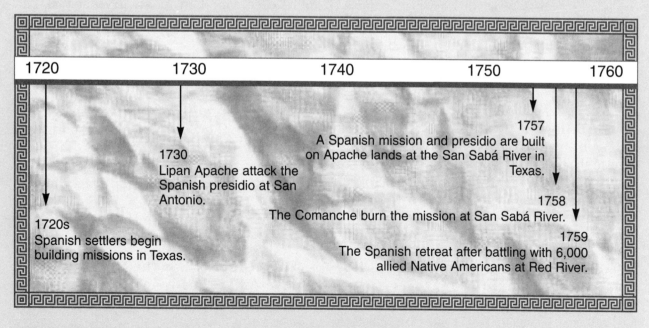

1720   1730   1740   1750   1760

1720s
Spanish settlers begin building missions in Texas.

1730
Lipan Apache attack the Spanish presidio at San Antonio.

1757
A Spanish mission and presidio are built on Apache lands at the San Sabá River in Texas.

1758
The Comanche burn the mission at San Sabá River.

1759
The Spanish retreat after battling with 6,000 allied Native Americans at Red River.

Once the Spanish decided to build settlements in Texas, they followed a plan they had used in other parts of the Americas. This plan had two parts.

First, Roman Catholic priests would build a mission in Native American lands. The **missionaries,** the priests who ran missions, tried to convince Native Americans to move into the mission. This made it easier to teach them about religion. But the missionaries also taught them European ways. Native Americans learned how to use European tools and raise European crops with European farming methods.

While the mission was being built, Spanish soldiers were building a **presidio** (pruh-SEE-dee-oh), or fort. The presidio and its soldiers would protect missionaries while the Native Americans were being converted. The Spanish soldiers could also help force Native Americans to stay at, and work in, the missions.

SECTION 1:
NATIVE AMERICANS RESIST THE SPANISH MISSION SYSTEM.

If all went well at the missions, the third part of the settlement plan would begin. This called for Spanish settlers to arrive and form a town near the mission.

The Mission System in Texas This mission system had worked well for the Spanish in New Spain. They had some success with it in New Mexico, just to the west of Texas, as well. But the system did not work as well in Texas.

Spanish missionaries in Texas expected the Native Americans to flock to the missions. This is what had happened in Mexico after the fall of the Aztecs. (See Chapter 1.)

In heavy armor, with a long-barreled gun that had to be rested on a long pole to fire, Spanish soldiers set out to control the American plains.

In Texas, things were different. Many Native Americans there were **nomads.** A nomad moves from place to place in search of food. Native Americans in Texas got their food by hunting and gathering. They did not want to live in one place the whole year round.

These Native Americans tried mission life for a while. But most of them found the work harsh and discouraging. They also saw many friends and family members die from European diseases at the missions. Many fled the missions to take up their old ways of life. The Native American populations at most Texas missions remained low.

Only one mission seemed to be doing well. The number of Native Americans living near the San Antonio mission was large. In this one place in Texas, the missionaries' plan of settlement seemed to work. However, the missionaries did not really understand *why* those Native Americans had come to the missions.

The Apache For the most part, the Native Americans living at San Antonio had not come seeking a new way of life.

THE COMANCHE AND THE SPANISH STRUGGLE FOR THE PLAINS

With horses seized from the Spanish, the Apache became feared warriors. Their raids forced other Native Americans to move to the missions.

They had come looking for protection. The danger they feared came from raids by other Native Americans, the Apache.

The Apache had once been nomads. They followed huge buffalo herds on foot across the Great Plains. The Apache used buffalo for food, clothing, shelter, and tools.

The Apache had long been raiders of settlements of other Native American peoples. When the Spanish moved into New Mexico in the late 1500s, the Apache raided their settlements as well.

From the Spanish, the Apache learned about horses. They soon were expert at riding and shooting arrows from the backs of the fast-moving horses. This skill helped them in hunting the buffalo. It also aided their war-making ability. Now they could range and raid over greater distances than before.

In the 1720s, a group known as the Lipan Apache began to move east into central Texas. Their raids led many Native American peoples to move closer to the walls and guns of the Spanish missions and presidios.

But the Spanish themselves were not completely safe. In 1730, for example, the Lipan Apache attacked the presidio at San Antonio. They killed 2 soldiers and wounded 13. They also captured Spanish cattle.

A Sudden Change in Attitudes The Spanish knew that if their settlements in Texas were to grow, there would have to be peace with the Apache. Spanish soldiers and officials wanted to make peace by defeating the Apache in battle. Spanish priests wanted to win the Apache over to mission life.

Neither the officials nor the priests got their wish. The Apache continued to mount stinging raids on Spanish outposts. They turned down all offers by Spanish priests to build missions in their lands.

Then, in the mid-1700s, things seemed to change. A Spanish priest reported what happened:

In March 1749, the Apache asked for peace. They ceased their warfare in the province of Texas. For almost a year they visited the presidio of San Antonio and its missions with much friendliness.

The Apache even told the Spanish priests that they wanted the missionaries to open a mission in their lands. The Spanish were overjoyed. It looked like years of hard work might be paying off.

In late 1756, a small group of Spanish soldiers and priests were ordered to build a mission and a presidio in Apache lands. The site chosen was the San Sabá River, almost 100 miles (167 kilometers) northwest of San Antonio.

Mission on the San Sabá In April 1757, five Spanish priests began to build the mission on the San Sabá. A small band of soldiers began to build the presidio about three miles (five kilometers) away.

But few Apache showed up at the mission. A disappointed priest wrote:

Most of the Apache stubbornly refuse to move to the mission. The few not opposed are so lukewarm toward the plan that I can hardly believe the promises they recently made. They told us that after their return from a buffalo hunt, they would come to the San Sabá River and live in the mission.

It took a while for the Spanish to figure out what was happening. The Apache had not suddenly been converted to the Spanish way of life. Rather, they were trying to build an alliance with the Spanish. They hoped to turn the power of the Spanish against a new enemy that had appeared. A new group of Native Americans had begun to press down on the Apache from the north. They were the Comanche.

Thinking It Over

1. Why was the San Antonio mission doing well?
2. Why did the Apache attitude toward the Spanish change in the mid-1700s?

SECTION 2:
THE COMANCHE RULE THE PLAINS.

The Comanche had begun to move south from what is now Wyoming about 1700. They, too, learned to use horses. Some got guns from French traders who had made their way west along the Missouri River. The Comanche soon became even more powerful than the Apache. Soon, the Spanish would learn to fear them.

The San Sabá River was near Comanche lands. That was the real reason the Apache had asked the Spanish to build a mission there. They hoped that the Spanish and the Comanche would begin fighting and kill each other off. Then the Apache would control central Texas again.

A Surprise Attack For almost a year, the San Sabá mission hung on. A few Native Americans would visit, but none would stay. From time to time, these Native Americans carried rumors of coming trouble. But nothing happened until March 16, 1758.

During the 1800s, the Comanche ruled the southern plains. Year after year, the Comanche swooped down on unprotected Spanish and Native American settlements. The Comanche were eventually conquered, not by settlers, but by disease.

That morning, a priest was saying mass in the mission chapel. Suddenly, calls of *"Indios! Indios!"* split the air. The priests rushed to the mission walls. There surrounding the mission were some 2,000 Comanche, armed with guns.

The Comanche rode up to the gates of the mission. They demanded to be let in. A Spaniard opened the gate. In an instant, 300 Comanche flooded in.

The Comanche began speaking angrily to the Spanish. They believed that the Spanish and the Apache were allies. Why else would the Apache have let them build the mission and presidio? The Apache were enemies of the Comanche. Therefore, the Spanish were enemies.

Suddenly, violence broke out. A gunshot killed a priest. A Comanche lance killed another priest. The frightened Spaniards took shelter in the chapel. Meanwhile, the Comanche burned the rest of the mission.

Word of the attack reached the Spanish soldiers at the presidio. A small band of soldiers was sent to rescue the missionaries. They rode straight into an ambush. Only one soldier survived.

The Comanche did not attack the presidio. Instead, they vanished into the Plains to the north. Behind them, they left in ashes Spanish hopes of expanding settlement through missions. Now, Spanish soldiers would try to take control by force.

Battle on the Red River The Spanish officials decided the Comanche had to be punished. They sent out a force that included Spaniards and Native Americans from other Texas missions.

The troops set out in August 1759. There were almost 600 soldiers, with two cannons and ample supplies. It was the largest Spanish force ever to enter Texas.

For almost two months, the Spanish tracked the Comanche northward. Then, on October 7, they found them near the Red River, near the northern border of Texas.

The Spanish expected to fight a running battle with Comanche mounted on horses. At the Red River, they got a surprise. One Spaniard told what they found:

> When we arrived at the Native American camp, we found it was well protected with trenches, a ditch, and a stockade. There were more than 6,000 Native Americans of different nations. They were all allied for the common defense and determined to shed their last drop of blood to keep us from entering the camp.

> The Native Americans had abandoned their ancient weapons, the bow and the arrow. They were now armed with rifles, swords, and lances, all of which they used with great skill.

The Spanish attacked the Native American fort but could not break through. They fell back in confusion. As they tried to regroup, the Native Americans charged out of the fort.

The Spanish troops began to retreat. Suddenly, they panicked. Abandoning their cannon and supplies, they fled south across the plains.

Weeks later, the survivors trickled into San Antonio. The defeat was one of the greatest the Spanish suffered at the hands of Native Americans.

A Milestone for the Spanish The defeats at San Sabá and the Red River were a milestone for the Spanish in Texas. The Comanche were too powerful. The Spanish made no more major efforts

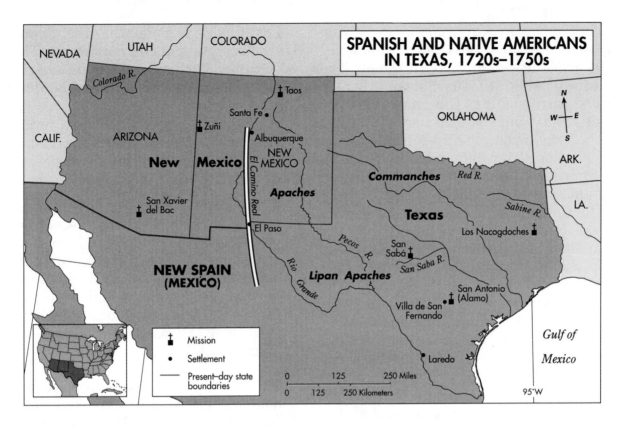

READING A MAP. What trail did Spanish friars and soldiers take to reach Santa Fe from Mexico? Which mission was located furthest east? Which mission was the furthest north?

to settle the province. Texas remained thinly settled until Mexico won independence from Spain in 1821. Then Texas became a part of that new nation.

By that time, people from the United States were looking hungrily at Texas. U.S. settlers would push over the border into Texas and rapidly outnumber those of Spanish descent living there.

The U.S. settlers would now face the Comanche and their allies. At first, the U.S. settlers had no better luck than the Spanish had. Most settlers gathered near the major villages so they could find safety from the Comanche in case of attack. Settlers on lonely farms lived in fear of Comanche raids. It took more than half a century before Comanche power was destroyed. Then the full power of the U.S. Army was launched against the Comanche. Even with all this force, the

U.S. at first could not defeat the Native Americans. It was only when a terrible outbreak of smallpox broke out that the Comanche were forced to give up. They ended their nomadic buffalo-hunting way of life on the Texas plains and were sent to live on reservations in the Oklahoma territory.

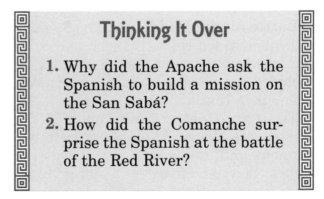

Thinking It Over

1. Why did the Apache ask the Spanish to build a mission on the San Sabá?

2. How did the Comanche surprise the Spanish at the battle of the Red River?

THE COMANCHE AND THE SPANISH STRUGGLE FOR THE PLAINS

CHAPTER 3 REVIEW

I. REVIEWING VOCABULARY

Match each word on the left with the correct definition on the right.

1. mission
2. presidio
3. nomad

a. a person who travels from place to place in search of food
b. settlement whose chief purpose was to convert people to Christianity
c. Spanish fort

II. UNDERSTANDING THE CHAPTER

1. Where was the most successful Spanish settlement in Texas?
2. Why did the Spanish build the San Sabá mission in 1757?
3. What Native American people were enemies of both the Spanish and the Apache?
4. What happened at the Red River on October 7, 1759?

III. APPLYING YOUR SKILLS

Main Idea and Supporting Detail Reread the section of the chapter that begins on page 29 with the subhead "A Sudden Change in Attitudes." (a) Restate the main idea of the section in your own words. (b) How do details in the section support this idea?

IV. WRITING ABOUT HISTORY

1. **What Would You Have Done?** Imagine that you are living at a mission in East Texas. Some Native Americans have come to visit the mission. Take the role either of a Spanish priest writing about the benefits of the mission or a Native American writing about the evils of the mission. Write a speech that one person might deliver to the other.
2. **Past to Present** Write a letter to a friend that compares the struggle among the Comanche, Apache, and Spanish with a struggle involving different nations today.

V. WORKING TOGETHER

Form into small groups. Use your school or local library to find out more about Spanish missions in what is now the United States. Construct or draw models of a typical mission for display in the classroom.

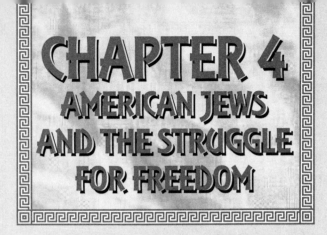

CHAPTER 4
AMERICAN JEWS AND THE STRUGGLE FOR FREEDOM

Jews in Spain suffered for their religion. Here a Jewish woman is condemned to be burned at the stake just for practicing her religion.

PEOPLE, PLACES, AND EVENTS

New Amsterdam
Francis Salvador
Jacob Henry

VOCABULARY

scapegoat
prejudice
synagogue

MULTICULTURAL MILESTONES

- Jews from Spain and Portugal arrived in the Americas.
- A number of Jews fought in the American Revolution.
- After the Revolution Jews won more rights.

PATHS TO THE PRESENT: SHIFTING BLAME

When things go wrong, it's hard to admit that the problem may lie with you, yourself. When troubles come to a person, it is easy to put the blame on someone else. It's a lot harder to take an honest look at yourself and admit you made a mistake.

Societies are not very much different from individuals. Often, when there are problems, society looks to blame a group that somehow differs from the majority. People in that group may be different because of how they look, the language they speak, or the religion they practice. When a person or group of people has been wrongly blamed, they are called **scapegoats.**

The people who have been made scapegoats may have made major contributions to society. But none of that counts when society is looking for someone to blame.

SETTING THE STAGE: EARLY REFUGEES

On August 3, 1492, Christopher Columbus sailed from Spain on a journey that led to Europe's discovery of the Americas. On the day before Columbus sailed, the last Jews were forced to leave Spain. They were expelled because of **prejudice,** not because they had done anything wrong. Prejudice is holding an unfair opinion about someone or something. During the 1300s and 1400s, violent mobs killed thousands of Jewish people. The mobs destroyed many homes and **synagogues,** or Jewish houses of worship. Other Jews were burned alive at the stake.

Finally, in 1492, the Jews were expelled, or forced to leave. Jewish refugees fled to many countries. Some Jews went to Holland, Italy, and the Ottoman Empire. Others sailed to Spanish and Portuguese colonies in the Americas.

The Jews who came to the Americas were among the first Europeans to settle there. Many Jews settled in the Portuguese colony of Recife (ruh-SEE-fay), in northeastern Brazil. In 1630, the Dutch seized Recife. The Jews of Recife prospered under Dutch rule. By 1645, almost 1,500 Jews lived in the colony. Recife's Jews brought the first rabbi to the New World. They also built a synagogue and a Jewish school for their children.

Unfortunately, these good times did not last. In 1654, the Portuguese reconquered Recife. Once again the Jews had to flee. Most of the Jews in Recife went to Holland. However, one group never left the Americas. This group of 23 ended up in the Dutch colony of New Amsterdam.

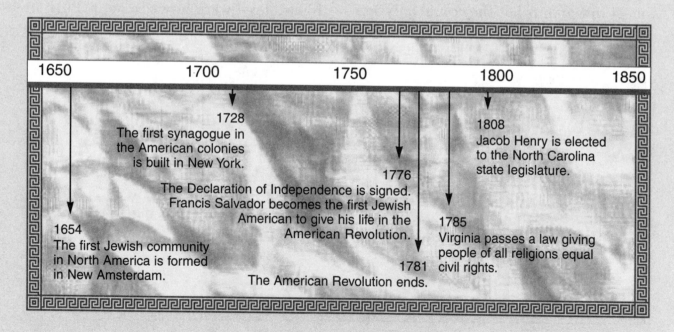

1650   1700   1750   1800   1850

1728
The first synagogue in the American colonies is built in New York.

1808
Jacob Henry is elected to the North Carolina state legislature.

1776
The Declaration of Independence is signed. Francis Salvador becomes the first Jewish American to give his life in the American Revolution.

1654
The first Jewish community in North America is formed in New Amsterdam.

1785
Virginia passes a law giving people of all religions equal civil rights.

1781
The American Revolution ends.

The 23 Jewish refugees arrived in New Amsterdam nearly penniless. New Amsterdam was on Manhattan Island in what today is New York City. Although the Jews were in a desperate situation, they soon became an important part of the colony. They formed the first Jewish community in what today is the United States.

The governor of New Amsterdam was Peter Stuyvesant (STEYE-vuh-sahnt). He did not want to allow the Jewish refugees to stay. But when the Dutch government granted Jews permission to stay, the governor had no choice.

SECTION 1:
JEWS CONTRIBUTE TO THE SPIRIT OF INDEPENDENCE.

Other Jews soon came to New Amsterdam from Holland. Although they could live in New Amsterdam, they did not have equal rights. They were barred from government jobs and from operating certain businesses. Nor were they allowed to have a synagogue. They could meet to worship, but they could only worship in their homes.

Asser Levy's Struggle One man who would not stand for this discrimination was Asser Levy. He was one of the original 23 Jews who had arrived in 1654. Levy decided to fight the rule that forbade Jews from becoming soldiers.

In 1655, Levy demanded "to be able to keep guard" with other citizens. His demand was refused. Yet he kept making this demand for two years until finally he won permission to defend the colony. Asser Levy continued to demand his rights. He became the first Jewish person to own a house in New Amsterdam.

In 1664, the British conquered New Amsterdam from the Dutch. By this time Levy was a successful businessman. He demanded equal rights from the British. In 1671, he became the first Jew in the British colonies to serve on a jury.

Jews in the British Colonies Like Jews in Spain, the Jews of England had long been persecuted. Only after 1657 were English Jews allowed to worship openly. Still, they faced discrimination.

This pattern continued in Britain's colonies in the Americas. During the 1600s, Jews were unwelcome in Puritan Massachusetts. However, they were

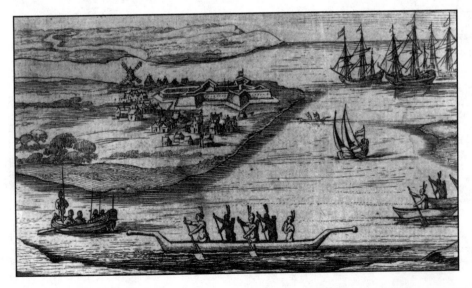

New Amsterdam, shown in this old print, offered some protection for Jews. In 1654, 23 nearly penniless Jewish refugees arrived in New Amsterdam and began to build new lives for themselves.

AMERICAN JEWS AND THE STRUGGLE FOR FREEDOM

On the eve of the American Revolution, there were small Jewish communities in such southern colonies as South Carolina. Here is the Beth Elohim Synagogue in Charleston as it looked in 1794.

allowed to settle in other colonies. Jews in the British colonies did not enjoy full rights as citizens. They could not vote in elections for colonial legislatures. They could not build synagogues.

Even so, life for Jews in the British colonies was far better than in most of Europe. More Jews therefore immigrated to Britain's North American colonies. They settled mainly in Rhode Island, New York, Georgia, Pennsylvania, and South Carolina.

Life for Jews in the colonies seemed to be improving little by little. In 1728, a group of Jews in New York received permission to build a synagogue. It was the first synagogue in the colonies. By 1760, the congregation was large enough to hire a Hebrew teacher.

Aaron Lopez's Success Story In 1763, Jews in Newport, Rhode Island, also built a synagogue. One of the leading members of the Jewish community was Aaron Lopez.

The Lopez family had come from Portugal. When Jews were being expelled from Portugal, the Lopez family remained. They practiced Judaism in secret for over 200 years. Then in 1752, Lopez fled persecution in Portugal and went to Newport. There he became a successful ship builder and trader.

When the 13 colonies declared independence from Britain, Lopez—like most Jews in Newport—supported the Revolution. During the Revolution, the British seized Newport. Aaron Lopez and a number of Jews moved to Massachusetts. You will read more about his contribution to the Revolution in the following section.

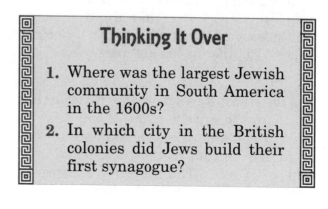

Thinking It Over

1. Where was the largest Jewish community in South America in the 1600s?

2. In which city in the British colonies did Jews build their first synagogue?

SECTION 2:
JEWS HELP FOUND THE UNITED STATES.

It was 1:45 AM on the dark moonless night of July 31, 1776. About 300 patriots rode quietly through the South Carolina countryside. Near the front of the group was 29-year-old Francis Salvador. Like his companions, Salvador had taken up arms to fight for independence. Unlike most of them, Francis Salvador was Jewish.

Francis Salvador: Patriot Between 1773 and 1776, Salvador had helped lead the resistance against the British in South Carolina. He served in two South Carolina congresses organized by patriots. He also helped write South Carolina's constitution and served in the state legislature. Later that year, he took up arms against the British. On this July night, he was on a mission to attack a British force.

Suddenly shots rang out. The unit had been ambushed. Salvador was hit three times and knocked from his horse. He lay bleeding until the battle was over. When the commander of the American forces came to him, Salvador asked if their side had won. "I told him yes," the commander remembered. Salvador said "he was glad of it, and shook me by the hand and bade me farewell." Later that night, Francis Salvador died, the first Jewish American to give his life for his country.

American Jews and the Revolution In 1776, there were about 2,500 Jews in the 13 colonies. They amounted to less than one percent of the total population in the colonies. The majority of Jews in the colonies supported the Revolution.

Displaying special courage under fire, Major Benjamin Nones helped lead American forces against the British in the southern colonies.

Jews throughout the colonies fought for their country. Isaac Franks of Philadelphia joined the rebel forces at the age of 17 in 1775. He served with George Washington at the Battle of Long Island. He was wounded several times and taken prisoner by the British. After the war, Washington at times stayed at Franks' home.

Another military hero was Major Benjamin Nones. He came to the United States from France in 1777. Nones began his service as a private and rose to the rank of major. After a battle in Georgia, the American commander cited Nones for

AMERICAN JEWS AND THE STRUGGLE FOR FREEDOM

"bravery and courage" and "daring conduct" under fire. Nones served with several important colonial generals during the war, including General Washington.

In South Carolina, almost every adult Jewish male in Charleston joined the militia. They fought at the Battle of Beaufort in 1779. The next year, they took part in the two-month long defense of Charleston.

Jews also fought in the militias of Virginia, New Jersey, Maryland, New York, and Pennsylvania. They fought in the Continental Army. Like Francis Salvador, some of them gave their lives so a new nation could be born.

Jews also supported the Revolution in ways other than fighting. Aaron Lopez and other Jewish merchants paid for some of the ships that ran the British blockade of the colonies. Those ships brought needed supplies to the colonies. The British Navy eventually captured most of Lopez's ships. As a result, he lost most of his wealth.

Haim Salomon also played an important role in the struggle for independence. He arrived in the British colonies from Poland in 1772. Salomon, who spoke ten languages, played a leading role in raising money for the Continental Congress.

The New Republic The Jewish community of the United States considered itself fortunate. All of the original states except Rhode Island, Connecticut, and Maryland guaranteed religious freedom in their constitutions. The U.S. Constitution guaranteed freedom of religion and allowed people of all religions to hold federal office.

In the summer of 1790, President George Washington visited Newport, Rhode Island. His visit was a chance for Newport's small Jewish community to express its feelings about their young country and its new President.

The Jewish community sent Washington a letter of welcome. They pointed out how in other countries Jews did not have the "invaluable rights of free citizens." However, in the United States there was a government "of the people." Other Jewish communities sent President Washington similar messages. Many American Jews believed that the United States was a country where they could live in freedom.

Fighting For Complete Equality Although they were free to practice their religion, Jews were not equal in many other ways. When the colonies won their independence, Jews enjoyed full equality as citizens only in New York. But most states did not allow Jews to vote or hold office. Some states did not openly exclude Jews from office. Instead, office holders had to take an oath stating their belief in Christian principles. The battle for equal rights was won step by step. In 1785, Virginia passed a law giving people of all religions full civil rights.

Several states soon followed Virginia's example. However, in some states the battle was more difficult. This was true in North Carolina and Maryland.

Jacob Henry After independence, Jews in North Carolina enjoyed religious freedom but not full rights as citizens. The constitution of North Carolina said that all office holders had to be Protestants. Despite that article, Jacob Henry was elected to the state legislature in 1808.

Henry was reelected in 1809. But then a political opponent challenged Henry's right to sit in the legislature because he

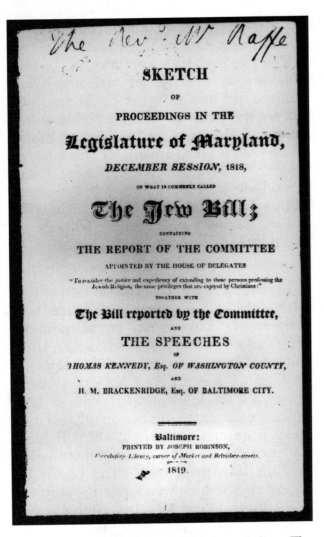

SKETCH

OF

PROCEEDINGS IN THE

Legislature of Maryland,

DECEMBER SESSION, 1818,

ON WHAT IS COMMONLY CALLED

The Jew Bill;

CONTAINING

THE REPORT OF THE COMMITTEE

APPOINTED BY THE HOUSE OF DELEGATES

"To consider the justice and expediency of extending to those persons professing the Jewish Religion, the same privileges that are enjoyed by Christians:"

TOGETHER WITH

The Bill reported by the Committee,

AND

THE SPEECHES

OF

THOMAS KENNEDY, Esq. OF WASHINGTON COUNTY,

AND

H. M. BRACKENRIDGE, Esq. OF BALTIMORE CITY.

Baltimore:

PRINTED BY JOSEPH ROBINSON,

Circulating Library, corner of Market and Belvidere-streets.

1819.

Maryland Jews faced persistent prejudice. The efforts of Thomas Kennedy, whose law is shown, gave Jews the same rights as other Americans.

was Jewish. Henry defended himself in a speech before the legislature. He said that the Bill of Rights protected freedom of religion. A person's religion was a private matter, "a question between a man and his Maker." Henry said that a person should only be punished "for what he does, and not for what he thinks." He added that persecution "in all its shapes" was against "the spirit of our laws."

Jacob Henry won a partial victory. The North Carolina legislature allowed him to keep his seat. This meant that other Jews could serve in the legislature. Henry's victory also opened the door for Catholics to hold office in North Carolina. North Carolina did not, however, change its law.

Religious Liberty in Maryland
Maryland also denied Jews equal rights as citizens. Its constitution required that an official declare "a belief in the Christian religion." In 1797, leaders of the small Jewish community in Baltimore asked that this article of the state constitution be changed. They said that Jews were denied "of the invaluable rights of citizenship" and asked to be put "on the same footing with other good citizens." Efforts to get the law changed failed several times.

Then Thomas Kennedy joined the battle. Kennedy was not Jewish. He was an immigrant from Scotland and a member of the legislature. He did not know any Jews personally. None lived in western Maryland where Kennedy's home was. That did not matter to Kennedy. He said that there were "few Jews in the United States" and "in Maryland there are very few." Still, "if there were only one, to that one we ought to do justice."

The struggle took eight years. Finally, a law passed in 1826 gave Jews equal rights with Christians in Maryland. Thomas Kennedy showed that fighting discrimination is not just a job for minority groups. It is a job for all Americans.

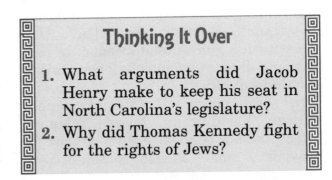

Thinking It Over

1. What arguments did Jacob Henry make to keep his seat in North Carolina's legislature?
2. Why did Thomas Kennedy fight for the rights of Jews?

CHAPTER 4 REVIEW

I. REVIEWING VOCABULARY

Match each word on the left with the correct definition on the right.

1. scapegoat
2. prejudice
3. synagogue

a. an unfair opinion about someone or something
b. a Jewish house of worship
c. someone who is blamed for the mistakes of others

II. UNDERSTANDING THE CHAPTER

1. What two important historical events occurred in Spain in 1492?
2. Why did the Jewish community of Recife have to leave that colony?
3. What was Peter Stuyvesant's attitude toward the first Jews who arrived in New Amsterdam?
4. How did Jewish Americans participate in the American Revolution?
5. Why did Jewish Americans have to fight for equal rights in the new republic?

III. APPLYING YOUR SKILLS

Using Chronology   Put the following events in chronological order.
a. Jacob Henry makes his speech to the North Carolina legislature.
b. Francis Salvador is killed in battle.
c. Jews arrive in New Amsterdam.
d. Jews are expelled from Spain.
e. Virginia grants people of all religions full civil rights.

IV. WRITING ABOUT HISTORY

1. **What Would You Have Done?**   Imagine you were a Jewish person living in the British North American colonies. Would you encourage other Jews to settle there? Explain your answer in a brief essay.
2. **Past to Present**   Write a newspaper article describing the contributions of American Jews to today's struggle for equal rights.

V. WORKING TOGETHER

Meet in small groups. Each group should use the school or local library to find out more about how members of an immigrant group took part in the struggle for independence. Select one person from each group to give an oral report about what you have learned.

CHAPTER 5
BERNARDO DE GÁLVEZ AND THE AMERICAN REVOLUTION

Latino troops commanded by Bernardo de Gálvez, at right on horseback, captured the important British post at Pensacola in 1781.

PEOPLE, PLACES, AND EVENTS

Oliver Pollock
Mobile
Pensacola

VOCABULARY

Patriots
neutral
blockade
rancho
vaquero

MULTICULTURAL MILESTONES

- Latinos led by Bernardo de Gálvez aided the American Patriots.
- Gálvez drove the British from the Mississippi Valley and from Florida.

PATHS TO THE PRESENT: MAKING TOUGH CHOICES

It's called "the lesser of two evils." You have two choices. Neither one is great, but one is worse than the other. So you pick the one that is "less worse." That was the choice that many Latinos in Louisiana and Florida made during the American Revolution. The American Patriots were fighting for their independence from the British king. Most Latinos did not support overthrowing any king.

*However, the Latinos disliked the power of the British even more than they disliked the idea of overthrowing a king. So they made a choice. They chose to side with the American **Patriots**, as the colonists who fought for independence were known. They then gave the Americans important assistance in winning independence.*

SETTING THE STAGE: A WIDER WAR

Battles at Lexington and Concord in April 1775 set off the American Revolution. That revolution spread from Massachusetts to the rest of Britain's colonies in North America. By 1776, all 13 colonies were fighting for independence.

The colonies had taken on Great Britain—the strongest nation in the world. Britain's armies had triumphed in battles all over the world. Its navy ruled the sea. Its trade and colonies had made it one of the world's wealthiest nations. If the colonies hoped to win their freedom, they would need help.

Fortunately for the Patriots, they got that help. Nations that Britain had defeated in earlier dealings welcomed the chance for revenge. At first, such nations offered money or supplies. In addition, volunteers from other countries fought with the Patriots.

As the Patriots began to win victories, some of those nations openly joined the fighting. The armies of France, Spain, and Holland began to battle the British. Some of the most important aid the Patriots received came from Latinos who lived in the Spanish colonies along the Mississippi River.

On a hot summer night in August 1776, a boat landed at the Mississippi River port of New Orleans. New Orleans in those days was the chief city of Spanish Louisiana. In the boat were 16 weary men. In just a few weeks of hard paddling, they had covered more than 1,200 miles (1,920 kilometers). The men in the boat were Patriots on a secret mission. They had come to seek help from the Spanish in Louisiana for their war against the British.

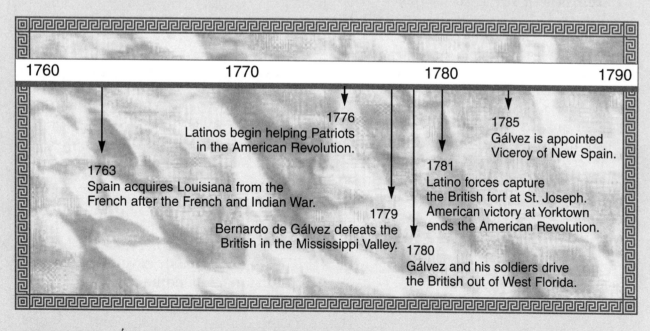

1760 — 1770 — 1780 — 1790

1776
Latinos begin helping Patriots in the American Revolution.

1763
Spain acquires Louisiana from the French after the French and Indian War.

1779
Bernardo de Gálvez defeats the British in the Mississippi Valley.

1780
Gálvez and his soldiers drive the British out of West Florida.

1781
Latino forces capture the British fort at St. Joseph. American victory at Yorktown ends the American Revolution.

1785
Gálvez is appointed Viceroy of New Spain.

Spain had taken over Louisiana only at the end of the French and Indian War in 1763. After Britain won that war, it took Canada from the French. It also took Florida from Spain.

In the complicated diplomacy of the day, another deal happened. To repay Spain for its loss of Florida, France gave Spain the territory of Louisiana.

Louisiana was a huge piece of land. It stretched from the mouth of the Mississippi north to the Missouri River. Then it turned west to the Rocky Mountains. Spain feared that Britain might one day try to force them out of Louisiana.

SECTION 1:
LATINOS JOIN THE EFFORT.

When the American Revolution began Spain was supposed to be **neutral** in the war. It officially supported neither side. However, Spain realized that if the Patriots won, it would lessen the British threat to Louisiana.

Patriots Ask for Aid The boat carrying the 16 Patriots gave the Spanish an opportunity. The leader of the Patriots, Captain George Gibson, carried a message to the Spanish. The message said the former British colonies had declared independence. The colonists pleaded for Spanish aid. They asked the Spanish for guns, gunpowder, and medicines.

The colonists wanted to receive these goods at New Orleans and take them up the Mississippi River. This would help them avoid British ships. British ships had **blockaded,** or closed off, the port cities through which most supplies arrived.

The Spanish response was to put Captain Gibson in jail. But this was only

Bernardo de Gálvez helped the cause of the American Patriots by removing the threat of a British attack from the Gulf Coast.

to fool the British. In fact, the Spanish gave 9,000 pounds (5,580 kilograms) of gunpowder to the Patriots. Gibson's men carried this with them as they marched back to the British colonies. The gunpowder reached Fort Pitt just in time to help turn back a British attack. Later, the Spanish sent another large shipment of gunpowder to the port of Philadelphia.

A Man of Action Spanish aid to the Patriots would soon increase. In January 1777, a new Spanish governor took over in Louisiana. His name was Bernardo de Gálvez (GAL-vez).

BERNARDO DE GÁLVEZ AND THE AMERICAN REVOLUTION

Gálvez was in his early 30s when he took his new post. He already had a brilliant military career. He had fought for Spain in Europe, Africa, and Texas.

Gálvez saw that helping the Patriots would also help Spain. It would remove the British threat to Spanish lands. It might also give Spain a chance to win back Florida from the British.

Under Gálvez, boats loaded with supplies made their way up the Mississippi to Patriot forts. He also protected Patriot ships that sailed to New Orleans. He would pretend to "seize" Patriot ships whenever British warships were nearby. When the British sailed away, he would release the ships.

Gálvez met secretly with Oliver Pollock. Pollock was a merchant who lived in New Orleans and supported the Patriots. Through Pollock, he arranged to send supplies and gunpowder to the Patriots. Gálvez also wrote letters to the Spanish king. In them, he urged King Carlos III to aid the Patriots. King Carlos agreed, and secretly sent large sums of money to the Patriots.

In 1777 and 1778, Gálvez was in contact with Governor Patrick Henry of Virginia. Henry suggested that Gálvez use the war to seize Florida from Britain. Gálvez did not need encouragement. He was already planning to attack Florida.

Three Forts Gálvez made his first target three British forts in West Florida. On August 27, 1779, he marched out of New Orleans at the head of some 660 men. Among them were Latinos from the Caribbean, Native Americans, Mexicans, 80 African Americans, and 7 Anglo Americans.

The little army trudged along through thick, hot forests. They slogged through swamps and streams. On the way, they passed through scattered settlements and asked people there to join them. Latino ranchers, German farmers, French trappers, and Native Americans agreed to join. When Gálvez's army

The busy city of New Orleans, at the mouth of the Mississippi, became the lifeline supplying U.S. Patriots in the west. Gálvez saw an opportunity to win back lost lands for Spain by helping the Patriots against the British.

reached the first British fort after 11 days of hard travel, it was more than double its original size.

The British had learned that Gálvez was coming. They had retreated to Baton Rouge. Gálvez quickly took the fort. Then he moved on Baton Rouge.

Gálvez knew that taking Baton Rouge would not be easy. The British had many veteran troops. They were well-protected. A deep ditch surrounded the fort. Inside the ditch were thick earthen walls and a high log fence. Behind the walls and fence were 18 cannons. The Spanish had only 10 cannons.

Gálvez believed that a direct attack on the fort would mean heavy losses to his force. So he thought of a way to fool the British. On the night of September 20, he sent a small group of soldiers to a small grove of trees near the walls of the fort. It was a natural place from which to launch an attack. The soldiers noisily chopped down trees, built walls, and fired muskets.

The British replied by moving their cannon around to face the grove. They opened fire and pounded it all night long.

Meanwhile, the rest of Gálvez's army was busy on the far side of the fort. As quietly as they could, they set up their cannon.

When the sun came up, the British discovered their mistake. But it was too late. The Spanish cannon soon battered a hole in the British fort. In three hours, the battle was over. The British commander surrendered. He also agreed to send a messenger to the third British fort calling on it to surrender.

Winning the Mississippi Valley In less than a month, Gálvez had dealt a stunning defeat to the British. He had captured three forts and more than 500 British troops. His losses were one man killed and two wounded.

Gálvez was now able to aid the Patriots in a major way. In May 1780, some 300 Latinos at St. Louis turned back a British attack. The British force was made up of 300 British troops and 900 Native American allies.

The Latinos were then able to march all the way north to the shores of Lake Michigan. In February 1781, they swept down on St. Joseph, a British fort on Lake Michigan. They burned the settlement to the ground and claimed the land for the king of Spain. The British army was not a threat in the western lands for the rest of the war.

Thinking It Over

1. Why did Bernardo de Gálvez want to go to war against Britain?
2. How did Gálvez's victory in the Mississippi Valley help the Patriots?

SECTION 2: LATINOS HELP WIN THE WAR.

Gálvez now turned his attention to the Gulf of Mexico. He began plans to capture the two chief British forts on the Gulf Coast, Mobile and Pensacola.

Planning a Strategy Gálvez knew that no army can survive without a supply line. A supply line is the way that food, ammunition, and other supplies are brought to a fighting force.

Gálvez knew that the American colonists did not have a good supply line. This was especially true for those who lived west of the Appalachian Mountains. Colonists there were cut off from the Atlantic coast for much of the year. In the spring, rain

BERNARDO DE GÁLVEZ AND THE AMERICAN REVOLUTION

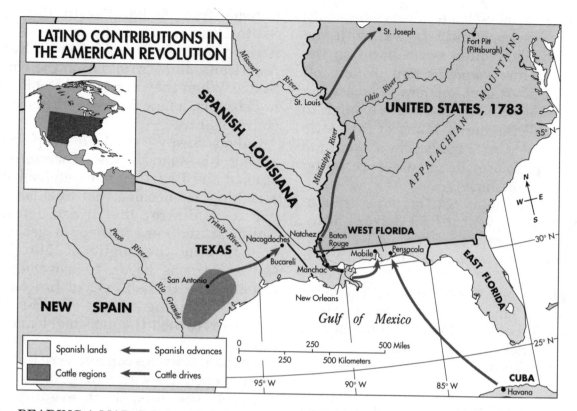

LATINO CONTRIBUTIONS IN THE AMERICAN REVOLUTION

Spanish lands
Cattle regions
Spanish advances
Cattle drives

READING A MAP. Gálvez aided the American Patriots in a number of ways. From what territory did he bring cattle? What was the most northern action taken by the forces under the command of Gálvez?

turned trails into mud. In winter, the trails were blocked by ice and snow.

The best highways west of the Appalachians were rivers. The best river highway was the Mississippi River. The river linked widely scattered Spanish, French, and American colonists, and Native American settlements.

The people who lived along the Mississippi and its many branches depended on the river for trade and transportation. New Orleans was therefore the most important city in the region. It linked settlements from Pennsylvania and Ohio to the Gulf of Mexico.

Supply Line from Texas Gálvez also knew that an army fought better if it was well fed. But Louisiana did not produce enough food to feed both his army and the

American forces in the west. He would have to look elsewhere for supplies.

Fortunately, Gálvez had served in Texas. He knew of the large herds of long-horn cattle that grazed at the missions and *ranchos* near San Antonio. A *rancho* is a farm where cattle are raised. Gálvez wanted to buy those cattle and bring them to Louisiana to feed his army and the Patriot army.

Hundreds of miles separated San Antonio and the Spanish settlements in Louisiana. How would the cattle get there? The *vaqueros,* or cowhands, from the *ranchos* would do the job. Those skilled riders would lead the herds across the plains and through the forests and swamps of East Texas to Louisiana.

Another problem was raids by the Comanche. The Comanche were skilled fighters on horseback. (See Chapter 3.) They were constantly at war with the Spanish. They often swept down on the herds, killing *vaqueros* and driving off cattle. Gálvez sent soldiers to guard the herds. But he could not spare enough to protect all the herds. Many of the cattle drives ended in tragedy. There were too few troops to provide complete protection from the Comanche.

However, many cattle got through. Some of them went to feed Gálvez's army. Much of the rest were sent to feed hungry Patriot forces in the American West. Between 1779 and 1782, *vaqueros* brought some 9,000 head of cattle to Louisiana. Thanks to them, the American Patriot forces would never be hungry as they attacked the British in the American West.

Moving on Mobile Now Gálvez was ready to attack Mobile. In January, 1780, Gálvez sailed from New Orleans with 12 ships. On board was a truly multicultural army. In its ranks were regular Spanish troops. But there were also vol-

unteers from Cuba, Puerto Rico, and Santo Domingo. In addition, there were African American volunteers, Native Americans, and Patriots from the United States. When they arrived at Mobile Bay in February, a new force of Cubans joined Gálvez's army.

Gálvez always tried to keep losses among his soldiers low. Therefore, he studied the British fort carefully before attacking. He decided that Spanish cannon could destroy the British defenses. But first the cannon had to get close enough. On the night of March 9, Gálvez's troops began to move up the cannon. The British opened fire on the soldiers, driving them off. But the Latinos returned the next night and the next.

By then, Gálvez's cannon were in place. They opened fire with a roar. All day they pounded the fort. That evening, the British called for a truce. Two days later, they surrendered.

A Bold Move Gálvez won more honor for the capture of Mobile. He was put in

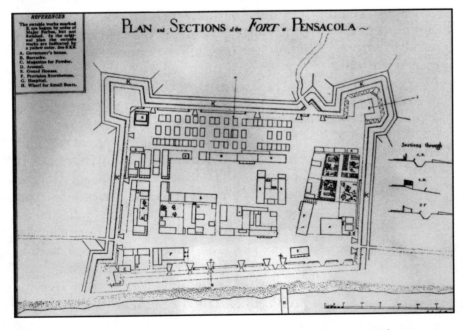

This diagram of the British stronghold at Pensacola shows the thick walls and commanding location. Why do you think the heaviest cannon were located on the side facing the bay?

BERNARDO DE GÁLVEZ AND THE AMERICAN REVOLUTION

charge of all military operations against the British in North America.

Gálvez was eager to press his attacks against the British. His next target was Pensacola, the capital of British West Florida. There, a well-protected harbor presented his toughest challenge yet.

Gálvez now had a large force of 64 ships and an army of more than 4,000. Yet the British were well protected. To take Pensacola, the Spanish ships would have to sail into the harbor. There, the ships' guns could protect the Spanish soldiers as they began the attack.

However, entering the harbor would be risky. Sandbars blocked much of the entrance. The guns of a British fort also guarded the entrance.

Gálvez ordered the Spanish admiral in charge of the ships to sail in. The admiral refused. It was too dangerous, he said. He did not want to risk his ships.

Gálvez was furious. He had four ships of his own that he had brought from New Orleans. He ordered his flag to be flown from the mast of the lead ship. Then the fleet fired a 15-gun salute. This was the sign that their commander was on board. The Latinos were daring the British fort to stop them. With his flag flying from the mast of the lead ship, Gálvez sailed into the harbor.

British cannons started firing at the four Spanish ships. Cannon balls cut through sails and lines. Amazingly, the ships made it through. Gálvez's army gave a mighty cheer as the ships dropped anchor in the harbor beyond the range of the British guns.

Soon, sailors on the other Spanish ships raised their sails. They, too, charged through the fire from the British fort and reached the safety of the harbor. As they did, Gálvez himself sat in a small boat, exposed to the British guns, and guided the ships past the hidden sandbars.

Victory By late March, Gálvez had his army ashore on the mainland. There his soldiers began to dig trenches and gun positions. These let them inch closer day by day to the British forts.

The British forts were stronger than any the Spanish had met thus far. British cannons blasted the Spanish. British soldiers attacked them again and again.

Gálvez, however, would not quit. If his troops were driven out of the trenches one day, they seized them again the next. They kept pushing those trenches closer and closer to the forts.

For 61 days, the Spanish attack went on. Their guns kept up a steady fire on the British. But their ammunition ran lower and lower. The Spanish began to use cannonballs the British had fired at them. Even so, by early May the Spanish had only a few days' supply of cannonballs left.

Then, on May 8, a Spanish shell hit the gunpowder supply in one British fort. A huge blast shook the fort, killing 85 men. The blast opened a gaping hole in the walls. Through it, Spanish soldiers poured into the fort.

With that fort captured, the Spanish had a perfect spot from which to fire on the other British forts. The British position was now hopeless. On May 10, the British surrendered. Gálvez had now retaken all of West Florida from the British.

After the War That fall, the Patriots fought their last major battle in the Revolution. After George Washington won the battle of Yorktown in October 1781, the British began to pull their troops out of what was now the United States of America.

For Gálvez, however, the war went on. In 1782, he led a successful attack against the British in the Bahamas. He was making plans to capture St. Augustine in Florida when the war finally ended in 1783.

The courage and military skill of Bernardo de Gálvez had meant much to the United States during the war. He had helped keep a steady stream of vital supplies flowing to the Patriots during some of their darkest hours. Furthermore, his attacks on West Florida had tied up British forces that might have been used to defeat the Patriots.

For Spain, Gálvez had eliminated the British threat to Louisiana. He had also won the lands of West Florida from the British.

Without West Florida, Britain decided that it could not hold East Florida. It returned that territory to Spain in the peace treaty ending the war. Gálvez thus had helped give Spain control of lands in North America that stretched from the Atlantic to the Pacific.

As a reward for his deeds, the Spanish king made Gálvez Viceroy of New Spain. This was the highest Spanish office in the Americas. Gálvez took over the post in Mexico City in 1785. A little over a year later, he died of a fever.

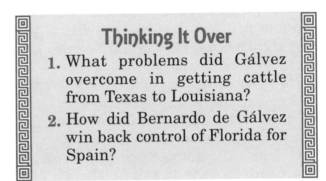

Thinking It Over

1. What problems did Gálvez overcome in getting cattle from Texas to Louisiana?
2. How did Bernardo de Gálvez win back control of Florida for Spain?

An old French print shows the defeated British army lined up on the shore at Yorktown ready to embark on ships for the return to Britain. The British defeat at Yorktown was the last major battle of the American Revolution.

BERNARDO DE GÁLVEZ AND THE AMERICAN REVOLUTION

CHAPTER 5 REVIEW

I. REVIEWING VOCABULARY

Match each word on the left with the correct definition on the right.

1. neutral
2. blockade
3. *vaquero*

a. to close off a place
b. cowhand
c. not taking sides in a conflict

II. UNDERSTANDING THE CHAPTER

1. Why did Latinos in the Spanish colonies help the Patriots?
2. Why did Gálvez want to seize British forts on the Mississippi River?
3. How did Gálvez get some of the food his army needed?
4. How did Gálvez win the victory that gave him control of all West Florida?
5. Why did the British give up East Florida after the American Revolution?

III. APPLYING YOUR SKILLS

Using Chronology On a separate sheet of paper, write the letter of the event that came first in each of the following pairs of events.

1. **A.** Gibson's mission to New Orleans **B.** Spanish takeover of Louisiana
2. **A.** Spanish raid near Lake Michigan **B.** Spanish capture of Baton Rouge
3. **A.** Battle of Yorktown **B.** Battle of Pensacola

IV. WRITING ABOUT HISTORY

1. **What Would You Have Done?** Suppose you were asked by the U.S. government to undertake a mission to win the aid of the Spanish. Write a message that Captain George Gibson might have carried to the governor of Louisiana asking for Spanish aid to the Patriots.

2. **Past to Present** The Latinos of Louisiana risked many dangers to give assistance to the Americans in their fight against the powerful British. Write a newspaper editorial supporting or opposing U.S. aid to a foreign country in the news today.

V. WORKING TOGETHER

Imagine that the Louisiana state legislature is deciding whether to declare a Bernardo de Gálvez Day. Break up into small groups. Make a presentation to the lawmakers in support of such a move. The presentation can be in the form of a speech, a videotape discussion, a collage, an advertisement, or any appropriate display.

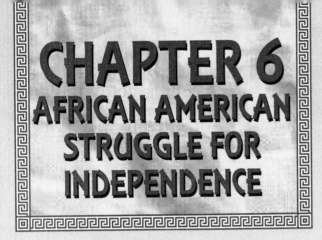

CHAPTER 6
AFRICAN AMERICAN STRUGGLE FOR INDEPENDENCE

At the battle of Bunker Hill, Peter Salem, a free African American, helped defend the hill and cut down the British commander.

PEOPLE, PLACES, AND EVENTS

Minutemen
Mum Bett

VOCABULARY

hypocrisy
Loyalists
petition
abolition

MULTICULTURAL MILESTONES

- Thousands of African Americans bravely served in the Continental army and navy.
- Mum Bett won her freedom in court. Her case put an end to slavery in Massachusetts.

PATHS TO THE PRESENT: LIVING UP TO IDEALS

Mum Bett was an African American who worked as a slave in the house of a wealthy man in Massachusetts. People in the house were always talking about freedom and liberty. Mum Bett could not help comparing their words with her status as a slave.

Have you had a similar experience? Many people are quick to "talk the talk," but do not "walk the walk." This is called **hypocrisy** *(hih-POC-ruh-see). Hypocrisy means pretending to be concerned about something you really do not care about at all.*

In a country that has as many high ideals as the United States, there are bound to be people who are hypocrites. They talk about high ideals, but they do not practice them in their lives. Mum Bett dealt with these kinds of people. She showed that to be true to itself, a society must practice the ideals that it preaches.

SETTING THE STAGE: REVOLUTION

By the 1770s, Britain was the strongest power in North America. Then, a challenge to British rule in North America arose. It did not come from another nation. Instead, it came from Britain's own subjects in its own colonies. Those 13 North American colonies had largely governed themselves for many years. But after its 1763 victory over France, Britain began to pay more attention to them, trying to tax them and control their trade.

The colonies protested, claiming that they were not represented in the British government. Therefore, the government should not tax them or control their trade. Slowly, the protests grew more angry.

When the American Revolution broke out, there were about 2.5 million people living in the colonies. About half a million people were of African descent. Most of them were enslaved.

At the start of the war, people in the colonies faced hard choices. About two fifths of the colonists supported the fight and welcomed independence. They were known as the Patriots. About a fifth opposed the war and wanted British rule to continue. They were the **Loyalists.** About two fifths of the colonists tried to avoid making a decision. They hoped to stay neutral.

The war that followed was the American Revolution. In it, the colonies won their freedom. A new nation, the United States of America, appeared. That nation spoke of new ideas of liberty and self-government that would inspire people around the world. As you will read, however, many people in the former British colonies faced a continuing struggle to enjoy that new idea of freedom.

1775	1780	1785	1790

1777
Vermont becomes the first state to outlaw slavery.

1784
Rhode Island and Connecticut end slavery.

1776
The Declaration of Independence is signed in Philadelphia.

1781
Mum Bett sues for her freedom and wins. Slavery is outlawed in Massachusetts.

1787
Richard Allen and Absalom Jones begin the Free African Society, dedicated to ending slavery.

1775
The Pennsylvania Society for Promoting the Abolition of Slavery is founded in Philadelphia. The American Revolution begins.

On July 8, 1776, a large crowd gathered outside the Pennsylvania State House in Philadelphia. Inside the State House, representatives of the 13 colonies talked about the war with Britain. That war had raged for over a year. Now, the representatives had decided on a bold move. The colonies would cut all ties to Great Britain. They would become independent.

The representatives had already approved and signed the announcement. Today, the public would hear it for the first time. An officer walked out onto a platform and began to read the Declaration of Independence.

"We hold these truths to be self-evident," the document announced, "that all men are created equal." The reader went on to tell the crowd that all people have certain rights, among them "life, liberty, and the pursuit of happiness."

When he was finished, the crowd burst into cheers. Cannons roared and church bells rang on into the night. Among those celebrating were African Americans, both free and enslaved. For them, the promise of liberty seemed especially sweet.

SECTION 1: AFRICAN AMERICANS FIGHT FOR FREEDOM.

When white Patriots used the words "liberty" and "freedom," they were talking about the kind of rights they wanted. For African Americans, liberty and freedom meant something else. These words meant an end to slavery.

African Americans listened carefully to both Patriot and Loyalist views. Patriots spoke most loudly of freedom and liberty. But some of the most famous Patriots, like George Washington and Thomas Jefferson, owned slaves. Loyalists, too, spoke of freedom. But some of the firmest Loyalists were Southerners who owned large numbers of slaves.

In the end, many African Americans worked and fought for the side that they thought offered the best hope of ending slavery. Some African Americans fought as Patriots. Others joined the British. Still others remained neutral.

In March 1770, the African American, Crispus Attucks, and four other colonists, were shot by British troops. This so-called "Boston Massacre" angered many people in other colonies.

AFRICAN AMERICAN STRUGGLE FOR INDEPENDENCE

Choices for African Americans

African Americans were part of the Patriot side from the beginning. Fighting in the Revolution began in April 1775 at the Massachusetts towns of Lexington and Concord. African Americans were among the Minutemen. These were Patriots ready to fight at a moment's notice. Peter Salem, Prince Estabrook, Lemuel Hayes, and Cato Woods were some of the African Americans, both enslaved and free, who battled the Redcoats and forced them to retreat.

African Americans also joined the bitter fighting at Bunker Hill, near Boston, two months later. Some 14 Patriot officers signed a letter that said,

> We declare that A Negro Man Called Salem Poor behaved like an Experienced Officer, as Well as an Excellent Soldier. This Salem Poor is a Brave & Gallant Soldier.

Joining Up In 1776, George Washington urged Congress to recruit African Americans for the army. Congress agreed, but said only free African Americans could join. As the war dragged on, however, more soldiers were needed. Soon, the Continental Army welcomed enslaved African Americans.

African Americans fought bravely throughout the war. Between 4,000 and 8,000 served in the Continental Army. Some 2,000 other African Americans serving on Patriot ships battled the British navy during the war.

Patriot leaders often praised these African American fighters. John Hancock, for example, hailed one company of African American troops from Boston for "their courage and devotion throughout the struggle."

Supporting the Patriot Cause Not all African Americans who aided the Patriots during the war carried guns. Some served the Continental Army as spies.

British officers bought enslaved African Americans as servants. Loyalist slave owners also loaned slaves as workers to the British troops. Some of these African Americans risked their lives to get news of British troop movements to the Patriots. In South Carolina, for example, Patriots praised the courage of a spy named Antigua in gaining "very important information from within enemy lines."

One of the most famous Patriot spies was African American James Armistead. Armistead worked in the Virginia camp of Lord Cornwallis, the British commander. Information that Armistead sent to the Patriots helped George Washington defeat Cornwallis at Yorktown, the war's last major battle.

African American women joined the effort. Some cooked for the soldiers. Others helped care for the wounded.

The African Americans who made those efforts hoped that such a victory would mean freedom for those who helped bring it about.

Fighting for the British Not all African Americans supported the Patriot side. A minister in Pennsylvania talked to two enslaved African Americans there. He noted, "They secretly wished that the British army might win, for then all Negro slaves will gain their freedom."

The British were quick to play on these hopes. In 1775, the royal governor of Virginia, Lord Dunmore, announced that any slaves of Patriot owners who fought for the British would be free. Hundreds of slaves slipped away from Patriot-owned farms and plantations to accept the offer. It was, in part, this response to Dunmore's offer that led the Continental Congress to accept African American soldiers.

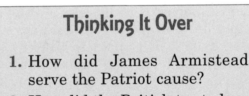

James Armistead risked his life to spy for the Patriots. Armistead gave information that led to the British defeat at Yorktown.

The British set up other units of African American troops. One company served at Boston. Another was formed in Philadelphia.

Winning Freedom Whether Patriot or Loyalist, all African Americans shared one hope. That was the dream that their service would lead to freedom. For many, that dream did come true.

The Patriots defeated the British at Yorktown in 1781. African Americans in the Continental Army began to leave it. Some had been slaves when they signed up. They had joined on the promise that they would be freed at war's end.

In most cases, slave owners kept their promises to African Americans and set them free. Where slave owners tried to go back on their word, state governments stepped in. Virginia, for example, passed a law giving the enslaved African Americans their promised freedom.

After Yorktown, British troops began to leave the United States. African Americans who had fought with the British often went along to freedom.

Some 20,000 African Americans left the United States after the war. But not all of them were free. Loyalist slave owners also left the country after the war. Many of them forced their African American slaves to leave with them.

Other African Americans also gained freedom after the war. They did so by seizing it, running away from their plantations and masters. Some fled to Canada. Others went to live with Native Americans.

African Americans who served in the Patriot and British armies had been fighting to win freedom for themselves. While they were, other African Americans were carrying on a struggle they hoped would bring an end to slavery completely.

Thinking It Over

1. How did James Armistead serve the Patriot cause?
2. How did the British try to lure enslaved African Americans to fight on their side?

SECTION 2: MUM BETT TAKES ACTION.

In a comfortable house in Sheffield, Massachusetts, a group of men gathered one January day in 1773. They talked over the problems that colonists faced under the British government. They also set

AFRICAN AMERICAN STRUGGLE FOR INDEPENDENCE

down on paper their ideas about what people should expect from their government.

The men paid little attention to a servant bustling about the house. She was an African American woman of about 30. Her name was Mum Bett. She was an enslaved person, owned by the owner of the house, Colonel John Ashley.

Mum Bett did her chores and said little. She appeared to show no interest in what the men were saying. But she was actually very interested. In years to come, she would use what she heard to work against slavery in Massachusetts.

Calling for Change There were many meetings like the one in Colonel Ashley's home during the Revolutionary years. At them, Patriots talked and wrote of the need for new kinds of government. Such governments, they said, should protect the rights of the people.

African Americans agreed. They believed that it was not enough for individual slaves to win freedom. The law should end slavery for good.

African Americans had been pushing for such changes even before the Revolution. Their chief tool was the **petition,** a written appeal to the government. African Americans filed dozens upon dozens of petitions with the governments of the colonies. After the Revolution, they filed these with the states. All pleaded with the governments to end slavery.

After the Declaration of Independence, the language of the petitions became stronger. They pointed out the hypocrisy of continuing slavery in a country that preached freedom.

In the Courts Some slaves fought against slavery in courts of law. Many individuals won freedom for themselves this way. Mum Bett did this in Massachusetts. But her case also helped

bring an end to the practice of slavery in the state.

Mum Bett worked in Colonel Ashley's house all during the Revolution. In fact, she and her sister had worked in the Ashley house since they were children. They were usually well treated. But Mum Bett knew they were slaves in a land fighting for freedom.

One day in 1781, Mrs. Ashley flew into a rage at Mum Bett's sister, Lizzie. She rushed at Lizzie swinging a heated shovel grabbed off the stove.

Mum Bett, enslaved in Massachusetts, challenged the system of slavery. Against all odds, she won and thereby ended slavery in Massachusetts.

To enslaved people, there was no more dreaded place than the slave market. Here, they were sent to strange places, split from families and friends, and condemned most likely never to see any of them again.

Mum Bett quickly stepped between the two. The blow aimed at Lizzie fell on her instead. It cut and burned deeply into her arm, leaving a scar that would remain for the rest of her life.

Mum Bett marched out of the Ashley home, swearing she would never return. She went to the office of Theodore Sedgwick. He was a lawyer who had taken part in many of the meetings at the Ashley home.

Mum Bett said she wanted to sue for her freedom. Sedgwick asked on what grounds. She reminded him that Massachusetts had adopted a new constitution the year before. This constitution said that all people were born free and equal. This is what she had heard the men discussing in the Ashley home while she was waiting on them.

Sedgwick took Mum Bett's case. Before the court, he argued that no earlier Massachusetts law had approved slavery. He added that, even if any such law had existed, the new constitution would overturn it. Mum Bett should be free.

The jury agreed. They said that Mum Bett "is not and was not the legal slave of John Ashley." The judge ordered Ashley to pay the costs of the lawsuit and an added sum as damages to Mum Bett. The result of Mum Bett's case was that slavery was no longer legal in the state.

The Struggle Widens Mum Bett's case was part of a new movement arising against slavery. The bravery of African American soldiers, the powerful petitions of enslaved African Americans, and news of court cases like Mum Bett's strengthened the idea that enslaved peoples had a right to freedom, too. A movement calling for the **abolition,** or end, of slavery was taking shape in the northern states.

Forced to labor long hours in the broiling sun, enslaved African Americans brought great wealth to the U.S. South through their labors. The South's economy was based on slavery and could not exist without it.

The first organization to work for abolition was founded in Philadelphia in 1775. Its name was the Pennsylvania Society for Promoting the Abolition of Slavery. By 1794, ten states had abolition societies. Many of these abolition societies were started by whites. African Americans were welcomed as members.

But African Americans started their own groups as well. In 1787, Richard Allen and Absalom Jones joined with six other African Americans to form the Free African Society. Members of the group promised to work for the end of slavery. They promised to

support one another in sickness, and for the benefit of their widows and fatherless children.

Other groups like the Free African Society started in New York City, Boston, and Newport, Rhode Island.

Limited Victories Slowly, antislavery ideas began to show some results. In 1777, Vermont passed the first law ending slavery. Pennsylvania followed in 1780 with an act meant to limit slavery. The Pennsylvania act did not do away with slavery immediately. Instead, it held that the children of slaves would be freed when they reached the age of 28.

Other states passed similar laws calling for a gradual end to slavery. Rhode Island and Connecticut did so in 1784. New York passed such a law in 1785. New Jersey followed a year later. As you have read, Mum Bett's case and another like it ended slavery in Massachusetts.

A Flawed Plan All the states that had outlawed or limited slavery were in the North. Would anything be done to limit slavery in the South?

During the summer of 1787, delegates met in Philadelphia to draw up a new plan for government. The result was the document we call the U. S. Constitution.

African Americans hoped the delegates would draw up a plan that put an end to slavery. They were bitterly disappointed when they saw the final document.

Growth of African American Population: Slave and Free, 1790-1820

	1790	1800	1810	1820
Enslaved African Americans	697,624	893,602	1,191,362	1,538,022
Free African Americans	59,557	108,435	186,446	233,634
Total	757,181	1,002,037	1,377,808	1,771,656

Source: the Negro Almanac: A Reference Work on The African American

To win the support of Southern delegates for the Constitution, Northern delegates agreed not to bar slavery. In addition, the slave trade from abroad could continue until 1808. At that time, Congress could end it if it wished. The Constitution also required the states to return runaway slaves to their owners.

At the time the new Constitution was being written, there were close to 750,000 African Americans in the United States. Eight of every ten of these African Americans were enslaved. For them, the Constitution seemed meaningless. The new plan of government did not "secure the blessings of liberty" for enslaved African Americans. Years of long, bitter struggle remained before that promise came true.

Mum Bett and W.E.B. DuBois After winning her case, Mum Bett changed her life. She started with her slave name. She changed her name to Elizabeth Freeman and went to work for the Sedgwick family. With the money she saved, she bought a small home in Stockbridge, Massachusetts. Later, she married. She died in 1829 at age 85. Among her descendants was W. E. B. DuBois. In the late 1800s and early 1900s, he would win fame carrying on the fight for equality that Mum Bett had taken part in long before.

Mum Bett left behind a moving statement that explained what freedom meant to so many enslaved African Americans:

Anytime while I was a slave, if one minute's freedom had been offered to me, and I had been told I must die at the end of that minute, I would have taken it. Just to stand one minute on God's earth a free woman. I would have done it.

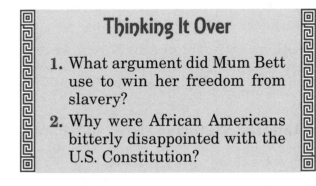

Thinking It Over

1. What argument did Mum Bett use to win her freedom from slavery?
2. Why were African Americans bitterly disappointed with the U.S. Constitution?

CHAPTER 6 REVIEW

I. REVIEWING VOCABULARY

Match each word on the left with the correct definition on the right.

1. hypocrisy
2. Loyalist
3. petition
4. abolition

a. a written appeal to the government
b. colonists who wanted British rule to continue
c. pretending to be concerned about something you really do not care about
d. movement calling for the end of slavery

II. UNDERSTANDING THE CHAPTER

1. Why did African Americans fight with the colonists in the Revolution?
2. Why did the Continental Congress welcome enslaved African Americans as soldiers?
3. Why did many African Americans leave the U.S. after the Revolution?
4. On what grounds did Mum Bett claim she should be free?
5. What did the Constitution say about slave trade from abroad?

III. APPLYING YOUR SKILLS

Supporting Generalizations A generalization is a broad conclusion based on facts that are related to each other. Read the generalizations below. Then skim through the chapter and write down two facts that support each generalization.

A. Many African Americans served the Patriot side bravely during the Revolution.

B. African Americans pushed for an end to slavery during and after the Revolutionary years.

IV. WRITING ABOUT HISTORY

1. **What Would You Have Done?** Imagine that you are an enslaved African American in 1775. You have just learned of Lord Dunmore's offer. Write a letter explaining why you would or would not accept it.

2. **Past to Present** You have just heard the details of the new Constitution. Write a speech to the delegates that predicts problems that Americans might still face two centuries later because of the failure to end slavery.

V. WORKING TOGETHER

Form a group with several classmates. Research a Revolutionary battle in which African Americans took part. Then draw an illustration of the battle, showing African Americans.

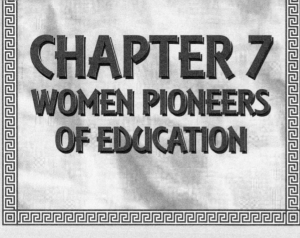

CHAPTER 7
WOMEN PIONEERS OF EDUCATION

PEOPLE, PLACES, AND EVENTS

Catharine Beecher
Hartford Female Seminary
Lucy Craft Laney

VOCABULARY

seminary
normal school
industrialization
urbanization

MULTICULTURAL MILESTONES

- Catharine Beecher devoted her life to spreading public education in the United States.
- Lucy Laney fought prejudice and established the Haines Normal and Industrial School in Augusta, Georgia.

"I was in the center of a wide Western Prairie." So wrote Arozina Perkins, who left the East to teach in a one-room schoolhouse made of sod, such as this Nebraska school photographed in 1886.

PATHS TO THE PRESENT: CHANGING ROLES OF MEN AND WOMEN

Make a list of teachers in your school. How many are men and how many are women? Did you know that before about 1830, it was not considered "proper" for women to be school teachers?

Today, the role of women in education is long and honorable. There are other professions where women have gained equal opportunities with men. Until a few years ago, women graduating from law school had trouble getting good jobs as lawyers. It was difficult for women to win entry into good medical schools.

All this is changing. It is changing not just because society's ideas have shifted. It took the sacrifices of many courageous people to make this a reality.

SETTING THE STAGE: EDUCATION FOR ALL

Before the 1850s, Americans did not generally accept the idea of a "public" school system. Public schools are schools supported by state or local government. Before this time, young people were educated at home or in village schools for which parents paid a small sum. Students learned basic reading, writing, and arithmetic. Children spent most of their time learning to farm or to take care of a house and family.

A few young men went on to private colleges. However, most men went no farther than the village school. Further education was not considered important for young women. Women only needed to know enough to read the bible, write a letter, and do simple arithmetic. But some women weren't satisfied with these limits. They wanted more, for themselves and for future generations.

The movement to bring women into classrooms began with a few determined women in the 1820s. Emma Hart Willard and Catharine Beecher started **seminaries** for female students. A seminary is a private school that provides specialized instruction.

Another movement tried to provide these women with ways of using their knowledge for the public good. Between 1846 and 1856, the National Board of Popular Education sent nearly 600 women teachers to the West to open schools. Their mission was to bring "civilization" to the frontier.

Most of these women were looking for ways to contribute to society. Many of them were looking for adventure or a place to call home. They were pioneers in the field of education.

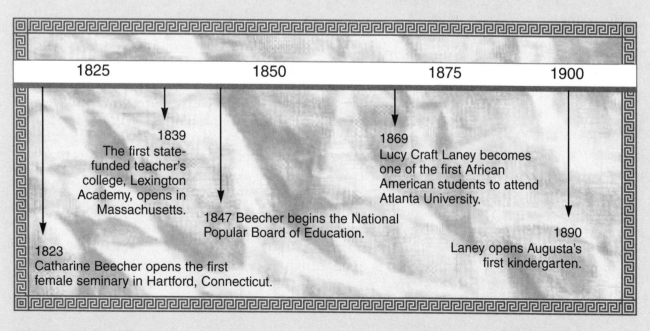

1825   **1850**   **1875**   **1900**

1839
The first state-funded teacher's college, Lexington Academy, opens in Massachusetts.

1869
Lucy Craft Laney becomes one of the first African American students to attend Atlanta University.

1847 Beecher begins the National Popular Board of Education.

1823
Catharine Beecher opens the first female seminary in Hartford, Connecticut.

1890
Laney opens Augusta's first kindergarten.

"I was in the center of a wide Western Prairie. One of the many dreams of my early days was about to be realized." So wrote 24-year-old Arozina Perkins in her diary in 1850. She had just arrived in Fort Des Moines, Iowa, to take up her position as school teacher.

SECTION 1:
CATHARINE BEECHER CRUSADES FOR EDUCATION.

Arozina was the youngest of twelve children. She had been teaching since she was 16 years old. Teaching was one of the few ways in which educated women in the 19th century could earn a living.

But Arozina dreamed of adventure. She wanted to devote her life "to the cause of education and truth and religion in the far west." For this purpose she was willing to travel six weeks by train, boat and wagon to a new and unfamiliar home. Once she arrived in Fort Des Moines, Arozina found herself teaching a class of 32 students ranging in age from five to thirty. She taught them all in a one room schoolhouse without adequate heating!

Arozina was exactly the type of young woman that Catharine Beecher was thinking of when she founded the National Popular Board of Education in 1847.

Pioneer of Teacher Training Beecher spent seven years traveling the West and raising funds for her project. She wrote articles and spoke at public meetings. Her message was simple and full of passion. The United States was neglecting two million of its children by not providing trained teachers. Schools in

Catharine Beecher, shown later in her life, devoted her career to building opportunities for women to become teachers.

Ohio, Missouri, Illinois, and territories further West desperately needed teachers.

Beecher believed these teachers should be women because women were "natural" teachers. She saw school as an extension of the home. There women were already responsible for early childhood training.

Beecher also believed that women should have the opportunity to become professional teachers. When she began her own teaching career in 1821, women were discouraged from being teachers.

Most Americans then believed that women did not belong in the classroom. There was no public school system. Schools were private and they were taught by men. These men were usually college students on their long winter breaks. Only men could go to college.

Women, if they had enough money,

could go to finishing schools. However, after school, they were expected to marry. Few people accepted the idea that a woman could actually have a profession outside of the home.

Beecher opened her first seminary in Hartford, Connecticut, in 1823. This school became the Hartford Female Seminary in 1827. It was a milestone in the history of women's education. Beecher insisted that women not just be taught domestic skills. They should also be educated in intellectual subjects. She also believed in physical fitness for women. She included daily exercise in the seminary's course of study.

This approach proved to be popular. The seminary grew from seven students to several hundred. It drew young women from all over the Northeast. By the time she was 28, Beecher was supervising a staff of eight women instructors.

Early Years The task of supervision came naturally to Catharine Beecher. Born September 6, 1800, she was the eldest of the eight children of Lyman and Roxana Beecher. As the eldest, Catharine was responsible for assisting in all household duties. She also had to care for her younger brothers and sisters. From this experience she learned at an early age the true value of work. She was also encouraged to take pride in her own abilities.

Lyman Beecher was a Presbyterian minister who became famous for his work in reform movements. Catharine's mother, Roxana, ran the household, taught school, took in boarders and even redesigned her own stove for better heating. These two caring parents had a strong influence on all the Beecher children. Catharine's brother, Henry Ward Beecher was a famous minister and strong opponent of slavery. Her sister, Harriet Beecher Stowe, became famous as an anti-slavery writer and author of *Uncle Tom's Cabin.*

Teacher and Writer Catharine also followed a writing career, in addition to her work as a teacher. For most of her life, she supported herself as a writer of pamphlets, articles, and books. She wrote textbooks on philosophy, domestic science, arithmetic, and physical education.

As a writer and a teacher, Catharine crusaded for the right of a woman to be treated fairly. Her goal was

to train a woman for teaching and then pay her so well that she can have a house of her own whether married or single.

Promoting the welfare of women was to be Catharine Beecher's life project.

Changing Times Fortunately, by the 1830s, other people began to see the need for women teachers. There was a movement in New England to create a public school system.

Like Beecher, the New Englanders believed that women were best suited to the role of teacher. But women needed training to make sure that children received a proper education. This led to the creation of the **normal schools,** or teacher's colleges.

The first state-funded normal school was the Lexington Academy, opened in Massachusetts in 1839. It had a class of 25 young women. They studied science, math, and philosophy. But the Lexington Academy also taught them how to be teachers. They stressed the skills that a good teacher must develop. These included knowledge, firmness, patience, self-control, and a deep interest in children.

The normal schools trained young women to provide a general education to all children. These schools marked the beginning of the teaching profession and public education as we know it today.

Thinking It Over

1. What was the purpose of the National Popular Education Board?
2. Why is Catharine Beecher's school considered a milestone?

SECTION 2:
A NEW AGE DAWNS.

By the middle of the 19th century, women had become accepted in the classroom. Between 1840 and 1880, the number of female teachers in the United States tripled. By 1880, 80 percent of all elementary school teachers were women.

The growth of teaching as a woman's profession owed much to the efforts of women such as Catharine Beecher. However, other events influenced this development as well.

New World, New Ways Throughout the 19th century, the United States was viewed as the land of opportunity for many people around the world. This led large numbers of people to immigrate to the United States. They were searching for new lives and better futures for themselves and their children.

These children increased the demand for teachers. Not only did immigrant children need to learn basic reading, writing, and arithmetic. Many needed to learn English as well. The demand for teachers led to more job opportunities for women.

Another event that increased the need for women teachers was **industrialization.** This is the process of developing factories, railroads, and other forms of industry. Industrialization created more job opportunities. Some of these jobs were open to women. They were mainly low-paying factory work. More importantly, industrialization created new and better-paying opportunities for men. This left the field of teaching, which did not pay particularly high wages, open to women.

Finally, the need for teachers was increased by **urbanization.** This is the movement of increased numbers of people into the cities, or urban areas. As factories and other industries grew, more people came to live in the cities. This meant more children were living in urban areas. In a farming community, these children could work on the land all day with their parents. In the new industrialized urban life, these children were often sent to school for all or part of the day.

Women's Work By 1850, the idea of women working outside of the home was no longer quite so revolutionary. However, there weren't many jobs open to women. They could work in factories, or as servants, or as teachers. A few women were breaking in to other occupations, such as medicine and business, but they were a minority.

For many women who had struggled to get an education, teaching became the preferred job. It was respectable, offered reasonable pay, and made obvious contributions to society. Teaching also allowed a woman to travel and to live independently. It had a certain social status. Most importantly, teaching offered single women at least some economic security.

Early in the 1800s, the study of medicine was closed to women. After the Civil War, women won the right to study medicine—but in all-female schools. This 1870 print shows students learning anatomy at the New York City Medical College for Women.

Civil War For all these reasons, many women in the 1860s and 1870s turned to teaching. But there were other reasons as well. During the Civil War (1861-1865) over half a million men were killed. Many educated women, left widowed or fatherless, turned to teaching as their only option.

But the Civil War also created new teaching opportunities. An end to slavery meant the chance for an education for many African Americans. Acquiring an education was now the goal for freed slaves. The need for teachers in the South attracted a new kind of pioneer woman. (See Chapter 14.)

Yankee School Teachers Groups were formed to promote education for the newly freed slaves. They sent teachers to the South to teach African Americans.

Most of these teachers were single women from New England. They were dedicated to carrying the principles of freedom to the war-torn South. One teacher wrote of the conditions under which she taught.

Can't buy anything on credit, and haven't a cent of money. The school shed has no floor. The rains sweep clean across it, through the places where the windows should be. I have to huddle the children first in one corner and then in another, to keep them from drowning or swamping.

Despite these hardships, northern teachers continued to go South, staying for a year, two years, or longer. By 1870, about 7,000 teachers were instructing 250,000 African American students of all ages. Eventually a new generation of teachers, both African American and white, arose to take over their duties.

Lucy Craft Laney The work of the northern groups continued in the South even after the northern school teachers were no longer needed. One of the ways the groups helped African Americans was by establishing high schools and colleges. One of the first African American students to enter the new Atlanta University in 1869 was 15-year-old Lucy Craft Laney.

Although she was born before the Civil War, on April 13, 1854, Laney never personally experienced slavery. Her father, David Laney, purchased his freedom as a young man. Then he purchased the freedom of his wife, Louisa. Lucy and her brothers and sisters were born into freedom. They had the self-confidence that freedom encourages. Said Lucy:

> I am as good as anybody else. God had no different dirt to make me out of than that used in making the first lady of the land.

There were other ways in which Laney was unique. Her mother taught her to read and write at age four. Further encouragement to learn came from her mother's employer who selected books for her to read. Laney would curl up in the big chair in the employer's library, reading books while her mother worked.

Starting School Laney's love of learning developed into a love of teaching. She graduated from Atlanta University in 1873. She spent the next ten years teaching in the public schools of Georgia. She opened her own school, in Augusta, Georgia, in 1886. It started with five students. At the end of its first year, the school had 75 students. By the end of its second year, enrollment had grown to 234.

Establishing and maintaining the school proved to be a difficult task. Funds were badly needed to expand and maintain the school.

Laney went to Minneapolis, Minnesota, in 1887 to the General Assembly of the church that endorsed her school. She was hoping to find support for her school. She had only enough money for a one-way train ticket. Despite her courage and perseverance, Laney failed to get the Church's financial support.

But at this assembly, Laney met Francina Haines. Haines proved to be a generous supporter of Laney's efforts.

She contributed funds and raised money among northern women to assist Laney. A grateful Laney renamed her school the Haines Normal and Industrial Institute.

Building for the Future Within a few years, the school had several modern buildings and several hundred students. Although the Haines Institute was co-educational, Laney had a particular interest in the education of African American women. She saw them as "the force that will uplift the Black race."

Throughout her career, Laney continued to break new ground for African American education in the South. She opened Augusta's first kindergarten in 1890. Two years later, she started a nurses' training course. Haines was the first school to provide athletic uniforms for girls and the first in Augusta to organize a football team.

Laney's goal was to produce well-rounded students who could contribute to the African American community. She wanted these students to be well-prepared as teachers in that community, or to be able to go to college. For these reasons, the Institute offered a full liberal arts curriculum. It emphasized high principles and strong moral character. Laney's primary goal, throughout her life, was to build character in her students.

Laney fought against racial stereotypes and restrictions. She saw children as the future of the country. As she said, "God has nothing to make men and women out of but boys and girls."

The Haines Normal and Industrial Institute survived well into the 20th century. By 1914, the school had grown to 900 students and employed more than 30 teachers. When Lucy Craft Laney died, at the age of 80, thousands of her former students mourned her passing.

The thirst for knowledge took in former slaves of all ages after the Civil War. Many women from New England went south to teach the newly freed African Americans and to train a new generation of Southern teachers.

Lucy Laney braved local prejudice and lack of funds to found the Haines Institute in Augusta, Georgia in 1886.

least in part, to the efforts of the women pioneers of education.

Thinking It Over

1. How did the Civil War help to expand teaching opportunties for women?
2. What role did Lucy Laney play in educating African Americans in the South?

The New Century By the turn of the century, women were firmly established as the teachers in the United States. In 1900, nearly 82 percent of all urban teachers were women. These women still faced many challenges. Women in all fields, particularly teaching, continued to be paid less than men in the same positions.

But many advances had been made in the 19th century. Women won the right to go to medical school and to study law. Women were admitted to regular universities and graduate schools in increasing numbers by the 1890s. In addition, they had established teaching as a recognized profession.

Women had not achieved full equality, but they were much closer than they had been a century earlier. This was due, at

CHAPTER 7 REVIEW

I. REVIEWING VOCABULARY

Match each word on the left with the correct definition on the right.

1. seminaries
2. urbanization
3. normal school

a. small private schools for women
b. teaching schools
c. the movement of more people into the cities

II. UNDERSTANDING THE CHAPTER

1. How did Catharine Beecher's upbringing prepare her for a career in education?
2. How did the industrialization effect women teachers?
3. Why did so many women become teachers?
4. How did the Civil War affect women teachers?
5. How did Lucy Laney's upbringing prepare her for a career in education?

III. THINKING ABOUT THE CHAPTER

1. **Drawing Conclusions** A conclusion is a statement supported by facts. Read the following statement, then list any facts that you can find in the chapter to support it: "Catharine Beecher was a 19th century woman with 20th century ideas."

2. **Using Chronology** Put the following events in chronological order: National Popular Education Board is founded; Haines Normal and Industrial Institute opens; Civil War begins; Hartford Female Seminary opens.

IV. WRITING ABOUT HISTORY

1. **What Would You Have Done?** Suppose you have been offered a position as a teacher heading west in 1850. Write an entry in your diary describing whether or not you would go, and your hopes, fears, and dreams.

2. **Past to Present** Based on the information provided in this chapter, how would you compare society's attitude towards women teachers in the mid-19th century to how we view women teachers today?

V. WORKING TOGETHER

Form a small group with several classmates. Call your local historical society and find out what you can about the first school in your town. Where was it? What kind of building did it have? Who ran it? Who was the first teacher? How many students attended classes? What was taught then? Locate where that first school was on a current town map.

CHAPTER 8
GERMAN AMERICANS: NEWCOMERS WHO OPPOSED SLAVERY

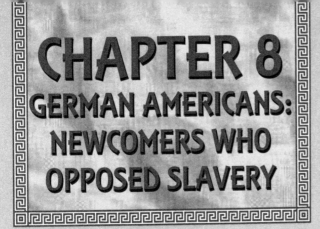

PEOPLE, PLACES, AND EVENTS

Gustav Koerner
Carl Schurz
Margarethe Schurz

VOCABULARY

inherit
reform
secede
kindergarten

MULTICULTURAL MILESTONES

- Many Germans came to the United States after the Revolution of 1848.
- The newly arrived Germans fought hard to prevent the spread of slavery to the U.S. West.
- During the Civil War, German Americans helped keep Missouri in the Union.

A bloody revolution in Germany, in 1848, aimed at setting up democratic government. When it failed, many Germans came to the United States.

PATHS TO THE PRESENT: FACING PREJUDICE

What is your experience with prejudice? If you have faced prejudice in the past, would you defend others who are facing it now?

Many German people who came to the United States between 1840 and 1865 had to answer that question. Many of them had fought in their homeland against wealthy land owners. They had fought hard for democracy. When their battles were lost, many were forced to leave Germany and come to the United States.

Here, they saw another injustice. It was called slavery. The story of how German immigrants united to fight the spread of slavery into the West is one of the great untold stories of our country.

SETTING THE STAGE: THIRST FOR FREEDOM

In the early 1800s, people in Europe began hearing about great opportunities available in the United States. They heard about great stretches of fertile land to farm. They heard about large cities where jobs were available.

These stories contrasted with life in Europe. Economic times were hard. Many workers could not find jobs. Farmers could not pay rent. Religious minorities often faced discrimination. By the mid-1800s, conditions got worse. Those who could afford the trip considered coming to the United States.

Other Europeans chose to come to the United States because they thirsted for freedom and democracy. In most of Europe, countries were led by rulers who **inherited** their positions. Inherit means to receive something when a relative dies. Europeans saw democracy working in the United States. Many wanted democracy in their own countries.

In 1848, a series of revolutions broke out all over Europe. These "Revolutions of 1848" were aimed at overthrowing old rulers and setting up democracies. Nowhere was this movement stronger than in Germany. In those days, Germany was divided into a number of small states. Each was ruled by princes, dukes, and other rulers.

The revolutions of 1848 failed, however. The revolutions were put down with much bloodshed. The fighting was particularly fierce in the German states. When the uprisings failed, thousands of people had to flee for their lives. Many came to the United States.

| 1845 | 1850 | 1855 | 1860 | 1865 | 1870 |

1848
Revolutions rage through Europe, sparking immigration to the United States.

1869
Carl Schurz becomes the first German American elected to the U.S. Senate.

1860
Abraham Lincoln is elected President of the United States.

1845
German American Gustav Koerner becomes a judge on the Illinois Supreme Court.

1861
The Civil War begins. German Americans help keep Missouri in the Union.

As a young man in Germany, Gustav Koerner dreamed about bringing democracy to his country. He fought for **reform,** or change, but was arrested by the government. After spending four months in jail, Koerner decided to move to the United States.

SECTION 1:
GERMAN IMMIGRANTS DEVELOP THE U.S. FRONTIER.

Gustav Koerner was one of hundreds of thousands of Germans who arrived in the United States in the early 1800s. Like many German immigrants, Gustav Koerner headed west. He settled in Belleville, Illinois, where he immediately threw himself into the politics of his new country. By 1845, he was a judge on the Illinois Supreme Court. He also served as Lieutenant Governor of Illinois.

Fighting for Democracy In Germany, Koerner had fought for democratic rights. In the United States, he saw injustice around him in the form of slavery. Koerner strongly opposed slavery. He joined the Republican Party in the 1850s. The Republicans were against allowing slavery to spread beyond the southern states.

In the election of 1860, Koerner supported Abraham Lincoln for President. Koerner made many speeches supporting Lincoln to German American audiences. Always he argued that slavery should not be allowed to extend into the U.S. West.

When the Civil War began, Koerner organized a regiment of volunteers to fight for the Union. After the Civil War, Koerner remained active in national politics.

Plans for a New Germany When the revolutions of 1848 failed to bring democ-

New York was the port of entry for most German immigrants. For those in this group, a long trip by train to Salt Lake City lay ahead.

racy to Germany, some German leaders planned to create an independent German state in North America. They considered various locations, such as Missouri, Texas, and Wisconsin.

Plans for an independent state did not work out, however. From the start, many Germans decided that they wanted to be U.S. citizens. They did not want a newly formed independent German country. They wanted to work hard and prosper within the United States.

One group of Germans from the German state of Bavaria settled in Missouri during the 1830s. They founded the town of Hermann, not far from St. Louis. In Bavaria, the settlers had planted grapes and produced fine wines. In Hermann, the settlers also planted grapes and made their new town a famous wine center.

Although the people of Hermann adopted many "American" ways, they did pay tribute to their German culture. They named the streets of their town for famous Germans, such as Beethoven, Goethe, and Guttenberg, the German who invented modern printing. German Americans of Hermann established singing groups and poetry societies. They blended their traditional German culture with their new life in the United States.

Earning a Living Many German immigrants became farmers. German farmers worked long hours on their land. They often bought farms from Americans who were moving farther west to the frontier.

Americans were impressed by how hard their new German neighbors worked. In 1835, a German farmer in Missouri wrote to relatives in Germany that he was building "a smokehouse, a kitchen, a milk-house, a stable for the horses, and one for the cows." He added that his "American neighbors say I am building a town."

Most states welcomed the hard-working German immigrant farmers. The newcomers were experienced farmers who knew how to choose good farmland. They were especially good at gardening, growing grapes, and raising livestock. They also were successful dairy farmers.

Germans who settled in western towns became important members of their new communities. Many towns in the United States had German grocers, butchers, and bakers. One German grocer in Ohio introduced his customers to a new breakfast food they had never seen. The food was dried oats, and became very popular. Today it is called oatmeal!

Joining the Military Many German Americans living in Texas served in the

This 1886 poster announcing a worker protest meeting is evidence of the importance of German Americans in the Chicago union movement.

U.S. army during the Mexican American War (1846-1848).

Sadly, like other Americans, German Americans who had fought on the same side during the Mexican American War, later fought on opposite sides in the Civil War. Louis Armistead, August V. Kautz, and Samuel P. Heintzelman were German Americans who served in the U.S. Army in the Mexican American War. Fifteen years later, in the Civil War, Armistead was a Confederate general. Kautz and Heintzelman were generals in the Union army.

Opposing Slavery Since many Germans had come to the United States to win greater freedom, they were opposed to slavery. Many German Americans rallied to the Union side during the Civil War. A total of about 180,000 young German Americans joined the Union army.

In 1861, southern states that permitted slavery were **seceding,** or withdrawing, from the United States. St. Louis, Missouri, was one of the first battlegrounds for the growing conflict against slavery. Missouri was a slave state and was thinking about seceding. Most German Americans in St. Louis opposed slavery. They also were against Missouri secession.

German Americans in St. Louis armed themselves to oppose the pro-slavery forces. A militia made up of German Americans guarded an arsenal containing guns and ammunition. Their actions kept these weapons out of pro-slavery hands. The efforts of German Americans helped Union forces control St. Louis, and keep Missouri in the Union.

Carl Schurz left Germany as a young man and became an American reformer and lawmaker. He was a leader of the anti-slavery movement.

Thinking It Over

1. Why did Germans come to the United States in the early 1800s?
2. Where did many Germans settle in the United States?

SECTION 2:
CARL SCHURZ FIGHTS SLAVERY.

In August 1852, Carl Schurz and his wife Margarethe sailed for the United States. The young couple had decided to leave Germany forever and make new lives in the United States.

Schurz in 1848 Carl Schurz strongly believed in democracy. Born in 1829, he was a student when the Revolutions of 1848 broke out. Schurz left his studies to fight for the revolution. He expected all of Germany to rise against their oppressors. In fact, most Germans did not join the uprising.

After some early victories, the tide started to turn against the rebels. In late 1848, Schurz led a military unit that was surrounded in a castle. Just as the castle was about to be captured, Schurz escaped by crawling through an underground sewer pipe.

The rat-infested pipe fed into the Rhine River. Schurz made his escape armed with pistols, two bottles of wine, and a string of sausages. He was a hunted fugitive for almost a year, until he escaped to London.

In London, Schurz met and married Magarethe Meyer in 1852. The Schurzes wanted to live in a democratic country. They did not believe they would ever have that chance in Germany. That is why one month after they married, Carl and Margarethe Schurz joined thousands of others in the long ocean journey to the United States.

To America Their boat left in August 1852. Schurz wanted to learn English as quickly as possible so he could take part in American life. On the journey to the United States, he spoke English whenever he could. As soon as he arrived in the United States, Schurz began reading English newspapers. He read every part of the newspaper, from the articles to the advertisements. Schurz also read books in English and spoke with people on the street. He learned very quickly. Within a few years, Carl Schurz became an outstanding public speaker.

The Schurz family settled in Watertown, Wisconsin. Carl bought a farm, but he was more interested in politics than in farming.

Because he strongly opposed slavery, Schurz joined the Republican party. He ran for the state legislature in 1856, but was defeated. The next year, Schurz was the Republican party's candidate for lieutenant governor of Illinois. However, he also lost that election.

Schurz was not alone. There was another Illinois Republican who lost an election during this time. His name was Abraham Lincoln. Lincoln and Schurz became lifelong friends and fighters against the spread of slavery to the western states.

Kindergarten While Carl was interested in politics, Margarethe was interested in education. In Germany, she had become interested in setting up pre-schools for young children. It was called **kindergarten,** or "children's garden."

In 1855, Margarethe started a kindergarten in the Schurz home in Watertown, Wisconsin. It was the first kindergarten in the United States.

The Civil War In 1860, Abraham Lincoln ran for President on the Republican ticket. Schurz fought hard to win votes for Lincoln. He gave speeches for Lincoln all over Illinois. After the election, Lincoln appointed Schurz U.S. ambassador to Spain.

When the Civil War started, Schurz begged Lincoln for the chance to return to fight for the Union. Lincoln granted his request. So Schurz gave up his high-paying, safe job for the dangerous life of an officer on the battlefield. He organized troops of German Americans and led them in campaigns throughout the South. After one battle he wrote:

> The stretchers coming in dreadful procession from the bloody field, their blood-stained burdens to be unloaded at the places where the surgeons stand with their bandages, their knives and their blood-smeared aprons, next to their ghastly heaps of cut-off legs and arms. And oh, the shrieks and wailing of the wounded men. There were the beseeching eyes of a dying boy who said with his broken voice: 'Oh, General, can you not do something for me?' I can do nothing but stroke his hands and utter some words of hope, which I do not believe myself.

A Political Career After the Civil War, Schurz continued his political career in Missouri. In 1869, he was elected to the U.S. Senate from Missouri.

THE LEVEE OR LANDING, ST. LOUIS, MISSOURI

St. Louis, shown here in the 1850s, attracted many new German immigrants. A thriving German American community led the opposition to slavery and helped keep the state of Missouri in the Union in the early days of the Civil War.

Schurz was the first German American elected to the Senate. In the Senate, he fought for reforms that would end corruption.

In 1877, Schurz became Secretary of the Interior under President Rutherford B. Hayes. In that post, Schurz fought for better treatment of Native Americans. He also was the first high government official to try to protect the environment of the United States. Like so many immigrants, Carl Schurz did not just become an American. He made our country a better place to live.

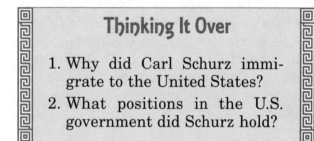

Thinking It Over

1. Why did Carl Schurz immigrate to the United States?
2. What positions in the U.S. government did Schurz hold?

GERMAN AMERICANS: NEWCOMERS WHO OPPOSED SLAVERY

CHAPTER 8 REVIEW

I. REVIEWING VOCABULARY

Match each word on the left with the correct definition on the right.

1. secede
2. kindgergarten
3. inherit

a. a pre-school for young children
b. to withdraw
c. to receive something when a relative dies

II. UNDERSTANDING THE CHAPTER

1. What were the Revolutions of 1848?
2. How did the Germans of Hermann, Missouri, blend German and American cultures?
3. Why did many German Americans oppose slavery in the United States?
4. What happened to Carl Schurz during the Revolution of 1848?
5. What was the role of Margarethe Schurz in American education?

III. APPLYING YOUR SKILLS

Using Chronology Put the following events in order, according to their dates:
- Carl Schurz comes to the United States
- Support from German Americans helps keep Missouri in the Union
- Pro-democracy movements grow in Germany
- German Americans play a role in the Mexican American War
- Revolutions of 1848 break out

IV. WRITING ABOUT HISTORY

1. **What Would You Have Done?** Imagine that you are Carl Schurz. You are being hunted throughout Germany. A friend hides you in her house. She urges you to stay in Germany and fight for democracy. Write a letter to her that explains what you have decided to do.
2. **Past to Present** Like Schurz, many Americans have come to the United States to escape oppression in other countries. Find someone in your community who has done so or find the story of a refugee in the newspaper. Write a list of questions that you would ask if you could interview the person.

V. WORKING TOGETHER

Meet in small groups. Use the school or local library to find out about how refugee groups have continued to fight for freedom while in the United States. Select someone from your group to give an oral report.

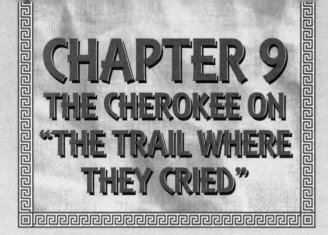

CHAPTER 9
THE CHEROKEE ON "THE TRAIL WHERE THEY CRIED"

PEOPLE, PLACES, AND EVENTS

John Ross
Indian Removal Act of 1830
Major Ridge

VOCABULARY

lobby
negotiate

MULTICULTURAL MILESTONES

- The pressure from settlers for land drove Native Americans off their homelands in the U.S. Southeast.
- Despite treaties upheld by the U.S. Supreme Court, the Cherokee were forced onto the "Trail of Tears" by the U.S. government.

Cherokee such as these young men, had built a thriving community in the U.S. Southeast before they were evicted from their homes.

PATHS TO THE PRESENT: KEEPING YOUR WORD

Trust is one of the foundations of society. If we do not trust the people around us to keep their word, we cannot lead secure lives. And if citizens cannot trust the word of their elected officials, they will lose faith in their government.

More than a century ago, the U.S. government signed a number of treaties with Native Americans. In most of them, Native Americans gave up their lands in return for promises of payments and new grants of land farther west. Most of these treaties were violated soon after they were signed.

The Cherokee, for example, saw treaties with the U.S. violated almost before the ink was dry. As you will read, these violations led to a very sad chapter in U.S. history.

SETTING THE STAGE: PUSHING BACK NATIVE AMERICANS

As the population of the United States increased in the 1800s, U.S. settlers pushed westward. Always, they found Native Americans living where they wanted to settle. In many cases, the Native Americans had already been pushed off other lands. In solemn treaties with the United States, Native Americans had handed over their lands. In return, they received new lands with a promise that they could keep them "as long as the rivers shall flow." But what were such promises worth?

Not much, as it turned out. Native American treaty rights were worthless unless the U.S government would enforce them against the claims of states like Georgia. Georgia argued that it owned all the lands within its boundaries. It said federal treaties that had promised vast areas of Georgia to the Cherokee were not valid.

U.S. President Andrew Jackson (1829-1837) agreed. Jackson supported a policy of "Indian removal" from the southeastern states.

This was especially bitter for the Cherokee. They had gone farther than any other Native American nation in adopting European ideas. They had abandoned a hunting way of life in favor of farming. Large numbers of Cherokee could read and write. Some had attended college. Many had become Christians.

The Cherokee put up strong resistance to losing their land. The story of their challenge to injustice is an important multicultural chapter in U.S. history.

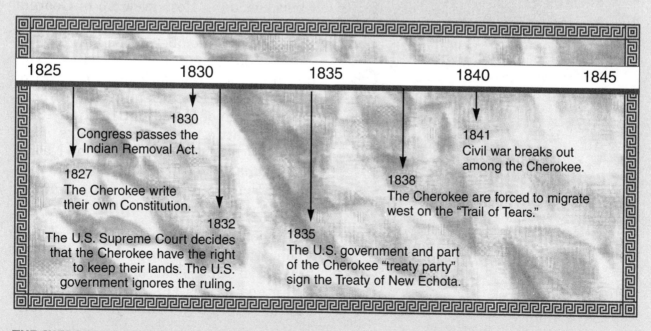

1825   1830   1835   1840   1845

1830
Congress passes the Indian Removal Act.

1827
The Cherokee write their own Constitution.

1832
The U.S. Supreme Court decides that the Cherokee have the right to keep their lands. The U.S. government ignores the ruling.

1835
The U.S. government and part of the Cherokee "treaty party" sign the Treaty of New Echota.

1838
The Cherokee are forced to migrate west on the "Trail of Tears."

1841
Civil war breaks out among the Cherokee.

THE CHEROKEE ON "THE TRAIL WHERE THEY CRIED"

John Ross was the principal chief of the 17,000 eastern Cherokee. He had traveled to Washington to try to convince U.S. government officials not to "remove" the Cherokee. Now, in the spring of 1833 he was returning to his farm in Rossville, Georgia. He was eager to see his family after being gone so long. He could not have guessed the scene he would find at home.

SECTION 1:
THE CHEROKEE FIGHT "REMOVAL."

Georgians had taken Ross's farm. They had taken his cattle and horses. They had even moved into his large home, leaving just two rooms for his wife Quatie and their children.

John Ross fought eviction and won his case in the U.S. Supreme Court. Ross was still forced to lead his people on the Trail of Tears.

Ross seethed with anger. For now, however, he could do nothing. He gathered his belongings and moved his family to another part of the Cherokee lands, on the border between Georgia and Tennessee.

From there, Ross led the Cherokee's fight to keep their land. Under Ross's leadership, the Cherokee sought their goals by peaceful means. They went to court. They **lobbied,** or tried to influence, the members of Congress. They appealed to the American public's sense of fair play.

Cherokee Leader John Ross showed how false was the widespread belief that Native Americans were "ignorant savages." In fact, he was better educated than most Georgians. As a boy, he had studied with a tutor. Later, he attended Kingston Academy in Tennessee. He spoke English better than he spoke Cherokee.

Ross had been active in Cherokee affairs all his life. Yet his parentage was a mixture of Scottish and Cherokee. His father, Daniel, had immigrated from Scotland. His mother, Mollie, was part Cherokee. John Ross grew up in Georgia surrounded by Cherokee. He was openly accepted as a member of the nation.

As a young man, Ross served as a soldier under Andrew Jackson in the War of 1812. He also fought against the Creeks in the Battle of Horseshoe Bend in 1814. In that battle, about 800 Creeks died. Ross saw how difficult it was for Native Americans to challenge U.S. soldiers on the battlefield.

Cherokee Culture and Government About the time Ross was fighting the Creeks, a Cherokee named Sequoyah invented a system for writing the Cherokee language. This system was officially adopted by the Cherokee in 1821. It was used, along with English, in a weekly newspaper called the *Cherokee Phoenix*. The *Phoenix* was published in the Cherokee capital, New Echota (eh-KOH-tuh), in northwestern Georgia.

New Echota was a center of Cherokee culture. As the seat of Cherokee government, it had many fine buildings. It had schools and churches. It had a Supreme Court building. There Cherokee judges settled legal issues.

In 1827, the Cherokee wrote a constitution. As leader of the Cherokee legislature, Ross helped to write the constitution. He was elected first principal chief in 1828. He was reelected many times, remaining in office until his death in 1866.

Land Losses The Cherokee had once claimed a vast territory in the U.S. Southeast. It covered what are now eight states. Over the years, in one treaty after another, the Cherokee lost more than nine tenths of their land. Their remaining land was in Georgia, Alabama, North Carolina, and Tennessee.

Ever since 1794, a trickle of Cherokee had been moving west across the Mississippi River. Some went voluntarily. Others were forced off their lands. Federal officials urged them to move west, into the northeastern part of present-day Oklahoma. By 1832, some 3,000 "western" Cherokee lived there.

Divisions Among Eastern Cherokee However, the main Cherokee leaders vowed to remain where they were. For many years, the 17,000 eastern Cherokee held their ground. But divisions slowly developed. Some Cherokee believed that it was useless to try to resist. They thought the Cherokee should make the best deal they could with the U.S. government. They should sign a treaty, sell their lands, and move west.

John Ross strongly opposed such a course. The Cherokee had made treaties before, only to see them broken. Why go through the same thing again?

Georgia's Actions Many Georgians desperately wanted the Cherokee land—especially after Cherokee miners struck gold on Cherokee territory in 1829. This sparked a gold rush. Georgia miners started swarming into Cherokee territory.

The Georgia legislature took matters into its own hands. It passed laws to take over vast areas of Cherokee land.

Indian Removal Act Meanwhile, Congress passed the Indian Removal Act of 1830. President Jackson strongly supported the act. It called for the removal of Native Americans from the Southeast. Besides the Cherokee, the act affected the Creek, Choctaw, Chickasaw, and Seminole nations. The U.S. government was supposed to buy land from "the five civilized tribes," as they were called. Then the tribes were to move west to the "Indian Territory" (present-day Oklahoma).

Within a few years, four of the five Native American nations signed treaties and moved west. Only the Cherokee held out. They decided to challenge the U.S. government in the Supreme Court.

States' Rights vs. Cherokee Rights In March 1832, the U.S. Supreme Court backed the Cherokee position. It said Georgia had no right to apply its laws to the Cherokee lands. The treaties between the Cherokee and the U.S. government were the "higher law." But Georgia

Forced by bayonets to leave their homelands, thousands of Cherokee moved west on the Trail of Tears in the 1830s. Almost 4,000 Cherokee died on the forced march to the "Indian Territory."

ignored the ruling. So did President Jackson.

The Treaty of New Echota Some Cherokee had decided to go against their leaders. Secretly, they made a deal with the U.S. government. In 1835, they signed the Treaty of New Echota. In exchange for $5 million and land in the west, the treaty turned over to the U.S. government all Cherokee lands east of the Mississippi.

Those who **negotiated,** or worked to settle, the treaty were known as the "treaty party." They were only a small portion of the eastern Cherokee. But they believed that what they were doing was right. If the Cherokee refused to negotiate now, they would have to move anyway. Georgia would take their lands for nothing.

However, the signers also knew that the treaty would infuriate most Cherokee. One of the signers, Major Ridge, knew that what he was doing was against Cherokee law. He remarked: "I am signing my death warrant."

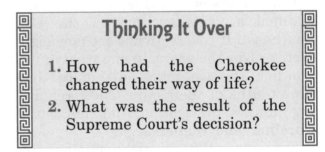

Thinking It Over

1. How had the Cherokee changed their way of life?
2. What was the result of the Supreme Court's decision?

SECTION 2: THE CHEROKEE TRAVEL "THE TRAIL WHERE THEY CRIED."

On a misty October morning in 1838, large numbers of Cherokee gathered at Rattlesnake Springs, Tennessee. U.S. soldiers stood guard. John Ross said a brief prayer. Then the group of 1,103 Cherokee climbed into their wagons. A bugle sounded and they set off toward the west. In the days ahead, 12 other groups under Cherokee leadership would start for the west. A total of 15,000 Cherokee would make the trek.

Ahead lay snowy mountains and icy rivers. The trip to Indian Territory would take three to six months. In the bitter fall and winter weather, one of every four Cherokee would die along the way. Later, Cherokee would refer to the roads they had traveled as "the trail where they cried," or "the trail of tears."

Trying to Defeat the Treaty Almost three years had passed since the signing of the Treaty of New Echota. During that time, Ross had worked hard to save the Cherokee lands. He had traveled back and forth to Washington, D.C.

Ross had tried to persuade the Senate to reject the treaty. In the end, however, the Senate approved the treaty by a single vote. It gave the Cherokee two years—until May 1838—to prepare. Then they would have to move.

Meanwhile, some 2,000 Cherokee moved west voluntarily. They included many of the treaty party. But the vast majority of the Cherokee stayed put.

Sending in Soldiers By 1838, the U.S. government decided to use force. General Winfield Scott led 7,000 troops into the Cherokee nation. At gunpoint, they rounded up Cherokee families and herded them into prison camps. Many died of disease while waiting to be sent west.

In the roundup, the Cherokee lost most of their possessions. Many saved only the clothes on their backs. Whites quickly moved in to take the Cherokee's homes.

The Way West The route west stretched for 800 miles (1,280 kilometers) or more. An observer near Little Rock, Arkansas, wrote: "Among the recent immigrants there has been much sickness, and in some neighborhoods the death rate has been great." Among the

dead was Quatie Ross, John Ross's wife. Even though she was suffering from a cold, she had given her blanket to a sick child. The child recovered, but Quatie died of pneumonia. She was buried along the Arkansas River.

The trip was heartbreaking for the Cherokee. One Cherokee recalled that

> People felt bad when they had to leave the Old Nation. A lot of us cried. We cried again on the inside when friends died. But we said nothing. We just put our heads down and kept on going towards the West.

Starting Over The Cherokee who made it to the Indian Territory had to start their lives over. But they had few resources.

For the first year, they depended on food supplied by contractors paid by the U.S. government. Some contractors cheated the Cherokee by keeping part of the food. Others supplied rotten food.

Having left their tools and seeds behind, the Cherokee had a hard time setting up farms. Ordinary Cherokee desperately needed their share of the $5 million the government had promised in the Treaty of New Echota. But political disputes held up payments.

Angry Disputes After all that had happened, the Cherokee people were sharply divided. About three fourths of the people looked to Ross as their leader. They agreed with him that the constitution of the eastern Cherokee remained in force. They believed all Cherokee should unite under that constitution.

However, western Cherokee (those who had come before 1835) already had a system of government. They wanted to keep that system and let the newcomers take part as equals. The "treaty party" of

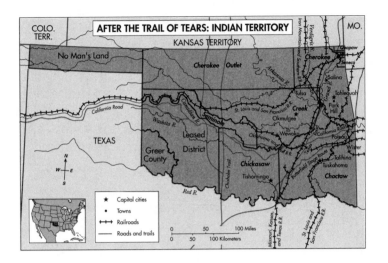

AFTER THE TRAIL OF TEARS: INDIAN TERRITORY

Reading a Map. What Native American group was located around the Town of Tishomingo? In general, which group lived further to the west, the Seminole or the Chickasaw?

Cherokee who had migrated between 1835 and 1838 sided with the western Cherokee.

Execution—or Murder? Under the laws of the eastern Cherokee, selling Cherokee property without authority was a crime. The penalty was death. To eastern Cherokee, the signers of the Treaty of New Echota were traitors. A hundred or so of the eastern Cherokee decided that the leading treaty signers had to die. On a June morning in 1839, bands of eastern Cherokee burst into the homes of those men in Indian Territory. They dragged the men from their beds and killed them. Major Ridge's prediction had come true. He was among the dead.

Civil War John Ross claimed he knew nothing of the plans for the killings. He tried to calm people down and get them to work together. But efforts to smooth things over failed. From 1841 to 1846, a civil war raged among the Cherokee.

In time, the war ended. The Cherokee rebuilt their homes, their farms, and their schools. They created a new capital that they called Tahlequah (TAL-uh-kwah). Prosperity returned for a time.

An Old Story After the Civil War, the westward migration of settlers put new pressure on Cherokee lands. Once again the U.S. government broke its promise. It forced the Cherokee and other Native Americans to give up more of their lands.

Then Congress declared the Native American governments abolished. It divided Cherokee land among individual Cherokee families. Settlers bought up the remaining lands.

Cherokee Today Since 1907, the Cherokee lands have been part of the state of Oklahoma. Tahlequah is still the Cherokee capital. After years of hardship, the Cherokee people have again begun to prosper. They are the second largest Native American group in the United States after the Navajos.

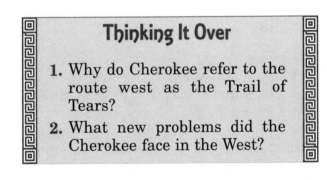

Thinking It Over

1. Why do Cherokee refer to the route west as the Trail of Tears?

2. What new problems did the Cherokee face in the West?

THE CHEROKEE ON "THE TRAIL WHERE THEY CRIED"

CHAPTER 9 REVIEW

I. REVIEWING VOCABULARY

Match each word on the left with the correct definition on the right.

1. New Echota
2. Tahlequah
3. lobby
4. negotiate

a. the Cherokee capital in Indian Territory
b. to work to settle a disagreement
c. the Cherokee capital in Georgia
d. to try to influence public officials

II. UNDERSTANDING THE CHAPTER

1. Why did the state of Georgia take over Cherokee lands?
2. What was the Indian Removal Act of 1830?
3. What was the Treaty of New Echota?
4. Why do Cherokee call their route to the West "the trail of tears"?
5. Why did quarrels break out after the eastern Cherokee reached their new homes?

III. APPLYING YOUR SKILLS

Identifying Points of View A French writer visiting the United States in the 1830s, commented on breaking treaties and policy of Indian removal: "Those who dishonor the law today will come to rue [regret] their actions another day." What did he mean?

IV. WRITING ABOUT HISTORY

1. **What Would You Have Done?** Suppose you are a Cherokee in Georgia. Major Ridge asks for your support in signing a treaty with the United States. He wants to give up Cherokee land in the Southeast in return for land in the "Indian Territory." Write a diary entry describing how you answered Major Ridge.

2. **Past to Present** The issue of trust in our leaders is of great significance today. Write a newspaper editorial relating the importance of trust in leaders with a national or local issue.

V. WORKING TOGETHER

Break up into small groups. Each group should create a poster about an aspect of Cherokee history from 1800 to the present. Make it part of a historical display for your classroom.

CHAPTER 10
THE BOY HEROES OF CHAPULTEPEC

Teenage Mexican cadets defended Chapultepec Castle from American attack. Rejecting surrender, the "boy heroes" paid with their lives.

PEOPLE, PLACES, AND EVENTS

Chapultepec
Los Ninos Heroes de Chapultepec
Treaty of Guadalupe Hidalgo

VOCABULARY

cadet
manifest destiny
expansionism
annex

MULTICULTURAL MILESTONES:

- The United States entered the war against Mexico to win large amounts of Mexican territory.
- The "Boy Heroes of Chapultepec" gave their lives to defend their homeland.

PATHS TO THE PRESENT: A DIFFERENT POINT OF VIEW

It is hard to understand how two people can look at the same facts and come up with totally different conclusions. But they do. We see this in our lives every day. We admire certain leaders and dislike others. Our friends may have just the opposite views.

U.S. history is no exception to this rule. Should California, Texas, and other Southwestern states be in the United States or Mexico? We may think that they were meant to be in the United States. But to the people of Mexico, these territories were taken unjustly.

The words of the U.S. Marine Corps anthem hail the troops that seized "the halls of Montezuma." Mexicans, however, remember another set of heroes. These are a group of Mexican teenage boys who gave their lives defending their country.

SETTING THE STAGE: MEXICO AND THE UNITED STATES AT WAR

The war between the United States and Mexico was one of the most bitter chapters in the history of the two countries. During the war, U.S. troops invaded and occupied Mexico. As a result of the war, the United States took half of Mexico's land. This covered the area of present day California, Utah, and Nevada, most of New Mexico and Arizona, and parts of Wyoming and Colorado.

Mexicans showed their bravery in the many battles against the invading U.S. troops. The Battle of Chapultepec (chuh-pool-tuh-PEK) was one of those battles. Fought on a hill right outside Mexico City, it was the last major battle of the war.

Chapultepec Castle was a military school for young men who wanted to become officers in the Mexican army. At Chapultepec Castle some students took up arms against the invading forces.

The young men who defended the castle knew that they were risking their lives to fight against the U.S. army. Six of them died in battle. We know them today as *Los Ninos Heroes de Chapultepec,* the "Boy Heroes of Chapultepec." Their heroic defense of the gates to their city gave them a special place in history.

In the United States we think of the war with Mexico as an overwhelming victory for the U.S. army. We rarely remember that many Mexicans died fighting to defend their country.

The story of the Boy Heroes of Chapultepec gives us another perspective on the war. It shows how hard Mexicans fought to defend their country. It shows that a struggle that one side may think is heroic may be considered evil by the other side.

1835	1840	1845	1850

1836
Texas declares its independence from Mexico.

1842
Chapultepec Castle is converted into a military school for young men.

1845
The United States annexes Texas.

1846
The United States declares war against Mexico.

1847
U.S. troops capture Chapultepec Castle.

1848
The United States and Mexico end the Mexican-American War with the Treaty of Guadalupe Hidalgo.

Young Juan Escutia could feel the U.S. artillery falling on Chapultepec. Walls and ceilings crumbled around him as he watched the invaders from his lookout post. U.S. troops were now at the gates of Mexico City. Although he was only a student, Juan was one of the bravest fighters defending the entrance to the city against the U.S. attack.

SECTION 1:
THE MEXICANS DEFEND THEMSELVES.

U.S. troops started their attack against Chapultepec Castle on September 12, 1847. The battle was one of the last before the final U.S. victory. Although the situation was hopeless, officers and students at Chapultepec made a last brave attempt to defend their capital city.

A Summer House The rocky hill of Chapultepec overlooks Mexico City a few miles from its main square. On top of it sits the Castle of Chapultepec. To both the U.S. and Mexican armies, Chapultepec Castle was an important location. It dominated one of the main gates into Mexico City.

We'll Stay and Fight! News of the approaching U.S. troops reached Nicolás Bravo, who was in charge of the military academy at Chapultepec Castle. He recommended to all **cadets,** or young army students, that they go home. He felt that the defense of the castle should be done by experienced officers. He also knew that the battle would be bloody and wanted to spare their young lives.

Some of the young cadets went home. But many decided to stay. Those who stayed knew that they were risking their lives.

After hand-to-hand fighting, with heavy losses on both sides, the Americans (right) defeated the Mexicans at Molina del Rey.

An Orphan from Chihuahua Young Agustín Melgar had no real home to go to. Both his mother and father had died. Still, he could have left. But, like many other cadets, he decided to stay and defend the capital of his country.

Agustín had a special reason to fight. His native city of Chihuahua (chuh-wah-wah), a few miles south of Río Grande, was one of the first areas occupied by the invading U.S. army. He felt that he was not only defending Mexico City, but also fighting to regain his native city.

Old Disputes The takeover of Agustín's home city was part of an invasion plan by the United States. Mexicans fought to defend their country and stop

THE BOY HEROES OF CHAPULTEPEC

the invasion. But by the time U.S. troops reached Chihuahua, they had already taken control of Mexico's northern provinces—California and New Mexico. The bravery of the Mexicans was no match for the strength of the U.S. army.

The U.S. invasions were part of a plan to get Mexican land. To the Mexicans, it was an unjust war.

The United States wanted to expand its borders from the Atlantic to the Pacific oceans. The United States called this **manifest destiny.** ("Manifest" means obvious) Americans argued that it was the nation's obvious destiny to grow westward.

Mexicans had a very different view. To the Mexicans the U.S. actions were **expansionism.** Expansionism is a policy under which one country expands by taking over the land of another country.

Months before the United States declared war, it had **annexed,** or added on, Texas. Texas had been part of Mexico. (See Chapter 3.) In 1836, Texas had declared its independence. Mexicans were angry when the United States annexed Texas. They also feared that the United States would not stop with the annexation of Texas. They believed the United States would now try to seize California and New Mexico.

When war was declared against Mexico, many U.S. citizens opposed the war. They felt that it was unjust. They also feared that it would add more slave-holding territory to the United States.

Mexican forces put up a strong fight against U.S. forces advancing from the north. This made the U.S. army think that it should attack from the east. Then it could head west to Mexico City. The invasion from the east started with a landing at the city of Veracruz on March 9, 1847. Commanded by U.S. General Winfield Scott, 10,000 men surrounded

Antonio López de Santa Anna was a talented military leader who first supported Mexican democracy, but later set up a dictatorship.

the city. The heavy bombardment killed hundreds of civilians. After a courageous defense, Veracruz fell. Scott was then able to march on to Puebla and wait for additional supplies before a final attack on Mexico City.

Mexicans would not make Scott's march to Mexico City easy. Along the way Scott would face thousands of Mexican troops under the leadership of General Antonio López de Santa Anna. Santa Anna's army was made up of very determined, but mostly untrained volunteers. After each defeat, Santa Anna would organize a new army of volunteers. Faced with a well-planned invasion, the Mexicans suffered great losses.

Last Stand After the seizure of Puebla, U.S. troops were right outside Mexico City. There was only one main holdout of Mexican defenses left: Chapultepec Castle. About 800 Mexican troops were defending the castle. Among them, the Boy Heroes would fight to the end. They understood that not just this hill, but their whole country was at stake.

As U.S. troops approached, Agustín Melgar realized that he was now alone in his lookout tower. He fired at the U.S. troops. Agustín left his position to find better protection. He was badly wounded, but from his new position he continued to fire. Finally, his wounds would not allow him to fire anymore. Two days later Agustín would be found dead.

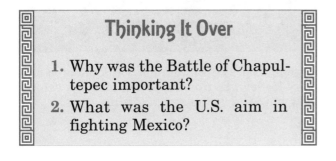

Thinking It Over

1. Why was the Battle of Chapultepec important?
2. What was the U.S. aim in fighting Mexico?

SECTION 2:
THE BOY HEROES FIGHT TO THE END.

Like Agustín, other cadets defending Chapultepec had come from parts of Mexico that were also under attack. They knew that many parts of their beloved country had fallen to the invading army. Vicente Suárez (SWAH-res) was from Puebla. U.S. troops were already in control of that city.

A Young Man with Experience Of all the young men who died defending Chapultepec, Juan de la Barrera (bah-REH-ruh) was the most experienced. At 19 years of age, he was also the oldest of the cadets. Juan had spent seven years in the army, having been allowed to join

when he was only 12. Juan received this privilege because his father was a general in the Mexican army.

When news of the invasion reached Mexico City in 1847, officers and students were asked to reinforce, or strengthen, the defenses around Chapultepec Castle. Juan's previous experience was valuable. He helped build defensive posts around the castle.

But there was no time to finish building the defenses. On September 12, the invading army was upon Chapultepec. By then Juan de la Barrera was a lieutenant. He was given command of the troops at his defense post. His troops protected the castle under a furious attack by General Scott's canons on the first day of the battle.

There were plenty of U.S. heroes at Chapultepec, as this U.S. print shows, but the Mexican "boy heroes" inspired their nation.

THE BOY HEROES OF CHAPULTEPEC

The next morning General Scott ordered his troops to storm the castle. They cut through Juan de la Barrera's defenses. Struck by a bullet, Juan died at the foot of the hill.

Look Out! U.S. forces cut through the defense lines and started climbing the hill that led to the castle. Vicente Suárez was standing guard on a lookout post. He could see the invading troops pouring over the castle, approaching his post. He warned others and then opened fire.

From his position, Vicente continued to fire at the advancing U.S. troops. But the troops kept on climbing the hill. The U.S. soldiers finally reached his position. There was a brief period of bitter hand-to-hand combat. Fourteen-year-old Vicente was killed by a bayonet in the combat.

The Youngest Loss Vicente Suárez was not the youngest student defending Chapultepec. One of his classmates, Francisco Márquez (MAR-kes), was only 13. Francisco entered the military school in February of 1847, a few months before the U.S. attack on Chapultepec.

Francisco was born in the city of Guadalajara (gwad-uh-luh-HAR-uh) along Mexico's Pacific coast. Francisco's father had died when he was a small child. His mother had then remarried a captain in the army.

Francisco fought back through the first day of the battle, surviving the heavy canon fire. On September 13, after U.S. troops stormed through the defenses of the castle, he was killed. His body was found at the bottom of the hill, torn by bullets.

Past Unknown Next to Francisco's body was that of Juan Escutia, one of his classmates. When the castle came under fire, Juan Escutia had only been a student for five days. His military record would have told us something about his life, but it was lost in the same battle where Juan lost his life.

Among the few things that we know about him is that he was born in Tepic (teh-PIC), a small town on the Pacific coast. Of all the students who died, Juan was the one who had entered the school last. In fact, he was not yet officially a student at the military academy. He arrived at the school a few days before the attack and his application was still being considered. Yet, like the others, he chose to stay after being offered the chance to go home.

Wrapped in a Flag As U.S. troops got closer to him, Fernando Montes de Oca (OH-cuh) reached for the Mexican flag and hauled it down. He feared that U.S. soldiers would seize it.

Fernando then wrapped himself in the flag, and jumped down from his position to continue fighting. He chose to die wrapped in his flag, rather than be captured. His body was found on the slope of the hill, next to that of Márquez. It was still wrapped in the flag he defended with his life.

Fernando died true to the words he had written on his application for the military academy:

I wish to serve and considering that our Republic has been invaded, I wish to be helpful in the present war with the United States.

The War Ends The U.S. troops had the upper hand. After two days of intense fighting, they took over the castle. The Battle of Chapultepec ended the war. To the sorrow of the Mexican people, their capital had fallen to the invading forces!

Each year, millions of Mexicans travel to the monument at the foot of Chapultepec Castle which honors the memory of the six young soldiers who gave their lives in defense of the castle.

After several months of occupation by U.S. troops, Mexico signed a peace treaty on February 2, 1848. It would be known as the Treaty of Guadalupe Hidalgo (gwah-dah-LOO-peh ee-DAHL-goh), after the village where it was signed. The treaty confirmed that Texas was now part of the United States. It also gave the huge territories of California and New Mexico over to the United States. In total, Mexico lost half of its land to the United States It would take many years of healing before the two countries would be the close friends they are today.

National Heroes Because of their youth and bravery, the Boy Heroes of Chapultepec are still remembered today with gratitude by the people of Mexico. They stand for the highest ideals of the Mexican nation. A very large monument to honor them was built at the bottom of the hill where they died.

Every year, on September 13, students lay flowers at the monument to the Boy Heroes. Their deaths are remembered with a public ceremony at the monument. A poem written by Mexican poet Amado Nervo is often read in their memory:

Como renuevos cuyos aliños
un cierzo helado destruye en flor,
así cayeron los Héroes Niños
ante las balas del invasor.

Like young flowers in bloom
destroyed by a freezing wind,
did fall the Boy Heroes
under the invader's bullets.

Thinking It Over

1. How did the Boy Heroes help their country?
2. What did the United States gain from the war?

CHAPTER 10 REVIEW

I. REVIEWING VOCABULARY

Match each word on the left with the correct definition on the right.

1. expansionism
2. annex
3. cadet

a. to add territory
b. a policy under which one country expands by taking over the land of another
c. a young military student

II. UNDERSTANDING THE CHAPTER

1. Why was the location of Chapultepec Castle important?
2. Why did the United States decide to invade Mexico from the east?
3. Who were the commanders of the two armies?
4. Why did the Boy Heroes decide to defend Chapultepec?
5. What is the Treaty of Guadalupe Hidalgo?

III. APPLYING YOUR SKILLS

1. **Reading for the Main Idea** Read the section titled "Old Disputes." Identify the main idea for each paragraph. Write them down on a separate piece of paper.
2. **Expressing an Opinion** Imagine that you're one of the survivors who defended the Castle of Chapultepec. Write a diary entry describing the events that took place on the last day of the battle. In your diary, be sure to give your opinion about the war between the United States and Mexico.

IV. WRITING ABOUT HISTORY

1. **What Would You Have Done?** Imagine that you are the U.S. Secretary of State at the time of the war with Mexico. The President has asked you for advice on whether or not to declare war. Write a letter to President Polk giving your best advice about the war.
2. **Past to Present** How has the relationship between the United States and Mexico changed from the time of the war to today?

V. WORKING TOGETHER

Meet in small groups. Imagine that you have been chosen to write a statement on a plaque in memory of the Boy Heroes of Chapultepec. Draw a model for such a plaque and write a statement for it.

CHAPTER 11
AH LUNG: THE POTATO KING OF CALIFORNIA

In 1885, white miners in Wyoming attacked Chinese mineworkers, killing 28 and driving hundreds of others out of the town.

PEOPLE, PLACES, AND EVENTS

Kwangtung
Chinese Exclusion Act

VOCABULARY

transcontinental
tenant farmer
yuen
fong

MULTICULTURAL MILESTONES

- Chinese Americans made important contributions to California's economy the 1800s.
- Ah Lung took land on the Sacramento River considered worthless and turned it into valuable farmland.
- The Chinese faced serious prejudice which they fought by banding together.

PATHS TO THE PRESENT: BEING DIFFERENT

It can be tough being different. We know this in our daily lives. People are usually not very friendly to strangers; especially if those strangers look different, speak a foreign language, wear different clothes, and have different customs and religious beliefs.

It was even worse for strangers back in the 1800s. Americans had not yet come to see that their differences were a source of strength. When workers from China started coming in large numbers to the Pacific coast states of California, Oregon, and Washington in the late 1800s, they faced a very lonely world. Sometimes, as you will read, that world was very hostile.

SETTING THE STAGE: BUILDING THE U.S. WEST

In the mid-1800s the United States was fast expanding westward. It was finding new riches and attracting new immigrants. The Gold Rush of 1849 brought people to California from the eastern portion of the United States. It also brought people from all over the world. Among them were thousands of Chinese who had made a long and dangerous journey across the Pacific Ocean.

Chinese pioneers had been arriving in small numbers to North America since the 1780s. However, the first large wave came in the early 1850s. They hoped to find gold in California.

U.S. leaders encouraged the Chinese to come. As the need for them grew, signs were posted in China, promising workers untold riches. One sign read: "Great Pay. Those who want to be rich come to the writer for a ticket to America. The details will be told on arrival."

Most of the Chinese came from the province of Kwangtung in southeastern China. Some expected to work in the United States for a while and then return to China. But many stayed.

With hard work and knowledge of farming, Chinese immigrants made parts of California into some of the best farmland in the United States. Chinese Americans also helped build the first railroad to join the east and west coasts. Many Chinese Americans became merchants. Some moved to other states.

Despite the many contributions of Chinese Americans, they were met with prejudice and discrimination. Ah Lung's story tells one person's struggle to overcome this discrimination.

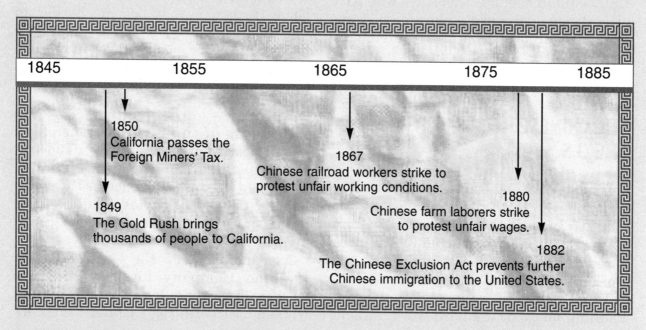

1845   1855   1865   1875   1885

1850
California passes the
Foreign Miners' Tax.

1867
Chinese railroad workers strike to
protest unfair working conditions.

1849
The Gold Rush brings
thousands of people to California.

1880
Chinese farm laborers strike
to protest unfair wages.

1882
The Chinese Exclusion Act prevents further
Chinese immigration to the United States.

Chinese workers for the Central Pacific braved rugged mountains and icy weather to finish their part of the transcontinental railroad.

The day Ah Lung had worked so hard for had finally arrived. Today he had signed his first lease to rent land in California. The year was 1898. It would take many more years before he could actually buy some land. But at least for now, he could rejoice. He would be able to work the land on his own and sell the crops.

Ah Lung, like many other Chinese immigrants, farmed the lands of California in the late 1800s. He was part of a larger migration movement from China to California that had started back in the 1850s.

SECTION 1:
THE CHINESE HELP BUILD
THE U.S. WEST.

When Ah Lung came to the United States in the 1890s, he was following the lead of many other immigrants from China. Their labor had given the Chinese a reputation as excellent and dedicated workers.

Many Chinese came to find gold. Panning for gold was hard work. Miners would have to find a place that looked promising along a river or stream. Then they would shovel sand from the stream into a pan. The sand was washed away, leaving behind heavier particles. They hoped some of these would be gold. Mining for gold meant long hours of work, usually with no return. Most of the time, the miners would find only worthless stones.

Gradually, the gold in the streams began to run out. It became harder to find gold this way. Then, the Chinese moved into other jobs. Some went to work in mines owned by others. Some went on to find jobs in other industries.

Builders of the Railroad One of the most important jobs the Chinese did was building a **transcontinental** railroad. Transcontinental means across the continent. In the United States, a railroad was built across the North American continent in the 1860s.

As early as 1865 the Central Pacific Railroad Company hired 50 Chinese workers. Two years later, 10,000 Chinese worked for the railroad. Chinese laborers were praised as hard working and productive. Yet, they did not receive free board and lodging. White workers did get these benefits.

The transcontinental railroad was completed largely because of the efforts of Chinese workers in the West and Irish workers in the East. But when the Chinese workers had completed their task, they lost their jobs. They had to find new work.

Fishing The long California coast offered the Chinese a way of making a living. Fishing was an old tradition among the Chinese immigrants. They brought from their villages in Kwangtung the knowledge they needed to start a fishing industry in California.

By the end of the 1860s, Chinese Americans had built a strong fishing trade in California. It continued to grow until the end of the 1800s. Chinese fishers caught many varieties that were used in Chinese cooking. Shrimp, shark, salmon, and cod made their way to San Francisco's Chinatown. Dried herring was sent to help feed Chinese working in the gold fields and on the railroad.

Through the years, the fishing industry expanded. By the late 1880s, Chinese worked in fishing from the state of Washington to Mexico. Chinese fishers helped introduce new seafood that changed eating habits throughout the United States.

Skilled Farmers Many of the Chinese had been skilled farmers in China. They now used their skills in California. Chinese farmers grew potatoes, oranges, cherries, tomatoes, and other fruits and vegetables.

As early as 1852, Chinese farmers worked for white landowners in the Sacramento area. These workers came from families in the south of China with a long tradition in farming. Back in China they had lived in the marshy lands of the Pearl River delta. In California, they used their skills to drain the land and build dams to control floods. They were able to turn the marshland of the Sacramento delta into rich farm land.

Using only shovels and wheelbarrows, the Chinese built dams to hold back the rivers. They built miles of irrigation ditches to channel water to the fields. Working waist-deep in water, they transformed what had been a swamp into one of the richest farming regions in the United States. Their top wages for this hard labor: a dollar a day!

The Chinese were so skilled at farming that they soon were in great demand in California. By the 1880s, almost 75 percent of California's farm workers were Chinese.

Some Chinese farmers developed new varieties of crops. One such variety was the Bing cherry, named after Ah Bing, the Chinese farmer who developed it in Oregon.

Because their skills were in demand, Chinese farmers were able to find work in other states. In Florida, Lue Gim Gong played a special role in helping build the orange industry. Today, people associate oranges and Florida. However, oranges are not native to Florida. They were brought to Florida by the Spanish. However, the fruit did not do well. The trees died when the weather turned cold.

Then in the late 1800s, Lue Gim Gong settled in Florida. He began to experiment with oranges. Lue bred various kinds of orange trees until he found one that produced juicy fruit *and* resisted frost. Without Lue's new variety of orange, Florida would never have been able to develop its giant citrus industry.

By 1880, Chinese made up 50 to 75 percent of agricultural workers in some parts of California. These Chinese are harvesting grapes in San Marino.

By the 1880s, the transcontinental railroad was complete. Now it was possible to distribute crops in large quantities to other parts of the country. In California, farmers had new markets. Many of them began to prosper. Ah Lung would be one of them.

Ah Lung's Potato Empire Ah Lung came to the United States when he was 19 years old. He had no money and very little education. Shortly after arriving in San Francisco, he got a job at a rice-importing store. He vowed to save all the money he could in order to own his own business.

Ah Lung's goal was to be a successful farmer in California. He prepared by spending his evenings studying English. The knowledge of English that he gained led to his first business opportunity.

According to California law, Chinese could not own land. So they had to rent it from white owners. A group of men from Ah Lung's village in China wanted to lease farmland near Sacramento. They would be **tenant farmers.** They would rent the land and pay the rent with a portion of the crops they grew. The rest would be profits.

However, none of the men spoke English. They invited Ah Lung to join the company and act as interpreter. The farm that the group leased prospered. Ah Lung saved every cent he could from his share of the business. He then invested that money in other businesses.

Ah Lung was able to save enough money to return to China and marry Leung Kum Kew. Back in California, Leung Kum Kew took in sewing in order to bring in more money. This allowed Ah Lung to lease more land.

Over the years, Ah Lung built a vast network of leased land in the Sacramento delta. Mostly he grew potatoes. He helped many new Chinese immigrants. He hired more than 500 immigrants and paid them well. Because of his great success, he became known as "the Potato King."

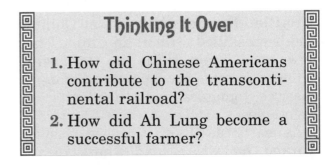

Thinking It Over

1. How did Chinese Americans contribute to the transcontinental railroad?
2. How did Ah Lung become a successful farmer?

AH LUNG: THE POTATO KING OF CALIFORNIA

SECTION 2:
THE CHINESE OVERCOME PREJUDICE.

Ah Lung had overcome hardship to succeed. Although he became wealthy, Ah Lung remained a tenant farmer. By the late 1800s, he and Leung Kum Kew had saved more than enough money to buy the farm they wanted. But events in California and the nation destroyed Ah Lung's dream of owning his own farm. The problem was prejudice against Chinese by whites.

Racism Against Chinese Prejudice against the Chinese had been present from the arrival of the first Chinese miners during the California Gold Rush. Chinese miners were often made to pan parts of rivers that were known to contain little or no gold. Later, Chinese workers on the railroads were given the most dangerous jobs.

When Chinese Americans began farming, farm owners took advantage of them by paying them low wages. This created resentment among white workers who felt that the Chinese were taking jobs from them.

Like Ah Lung, many Chinese farmers didn't want to work other people's land. They wanted farms of their own.

Anti-Chinese Riots Prejudice soon led to anti-Chinese riots in California. White people from rural areas raided farms that hired Chinese laborers. Chinese workers were forced to move back to San Francisco. The violence spread to the cities. There, raiders destroyed the homes of Chinese immigrants and looted their stores.

The Workingmen's Party A new political party promoted anti-Chinese feelings. The Workingman's Party pretended to defend workers' rights. However, the party was in fact against foreigners, especially the Chinese.

Unfair Laws The Chinese hoped the law would protect them, but they were disappointed. The law was on the rioters' side. California and Oregon started to pass laws that discriminated against the Chinese.

Unlike other miners in the California goldfields, Chinese miners worked together and helped one another in times of trouble. There was plenty of trouble, as the Chinese faced widespread discrimination and, sometimes, violence.

AH LUNG: THE POTATO KING OF CALIFORNIA

101

Anti-Chinese feeling in the United States led to passage of a law that required Chinese living in the U.S. to carry certificates of residence like the one shown here.

One early example was the California Foreign Miners' Tax of 1850. It forced foreign miners to pay a high monthly fee for the opportunity to mine, whether they found any gold or not. It was used first against Mexicans. Two years later, the state of California used it again against the Chinese.

At the same time, Chinese were forced to remain foreigners. They were barred from becoming U.S. citizens by a 1790 federal law. This law allowed only white people to become U.S. citizens.

Things got worse in 1882, when the U.S. Congress passed the Chinese Exclusion Act. According to this law, Chinese laborers were no longer allowed to come to the United States. Teachers and merchants could come, but they were still not allowed to become U.S. citizens. Six years later, another law prohibited the return of more than 20,000 Chinese laborers who lived in the U.S. and had gone to visit their families in China.

No Land for Foreigners These unfair laws continued well into the 1900s. They prevented Ah Lung's dream from coming true. California passed a law called the Alien Land Act, which said that only those who could become citizens could own land in the state. Since the Chinese were barred from becoming citizens, they were prevented from owning land in California.

Ah Lung refused to give up his dream. He went to Oregon and bought land there. He also turned to other businesses. He began an import business in San Francisco. By now, he was very wealthy. But Ah Lung's wealth could not protect him or his family from discrimination.

In 1923, Oregon passed a law similar to California's. Soon after that, Ah Lung began buying land in China. In time, he turned over his U.S. businesses to his sons and returned to China.

Fighting Back In spite of the difficulties, Chinese Americans helped each other

AH LUNG: THE POTATO KING OF CALIFORNIA

survive. Instead of quietly accepting mistreatment, they fought for their rights.

Many protests were organized by Chinese workers to demand better working conditions. In 1867, Chinese working on the transcontinental railroad dropped their picks and shovels, bringing work to a halt. They had much to complain about: long hours, low pay, and the harsh treatment from overseers. But the railroad company had the power to cut off their supplies and force them to go back to work or starve.

Farm laborers too revolted against the unfair practices. One of those protests took place in 1880. Chinese produce pickers in Santa Clara organized a strike to demand better pay. The workers knew that they were worth more than they were being paid.

Chinese farmers created their own organizations to help and protect themselves. Many, like Ah Lung, wanted to become tenant farmers. For that they needed money. Saving money took a long time, so Chinese Americans created organizations that could lend farmers the money to lease their own piece of land.

Chinese tenant farmers also developed **yuens,** or cooperative farming companies. Members of a *yuen* put together their resources to lease and operate their farms. Each partner had a share of the farm. Ah Lung was one of these early tenant farmers.

Refuge in the Cities Over the years, the Chinese population in the cities grew. There were neighborhoods where many Chinese families lived together. These neighborhoods came to be known as "Chinatowns." Chinatown provided its people with services and a sense of security. The largest Chinatown developed in San Francisco. Other cities in the West,

such as Los Angeles and Sacramento, developed their own Chinatowns, too.

Chinatowns were bustling business centers. Stores in San Francisco's Chinatown provided all kinds of goods and services. Brightly colored signs with Chinese characters marked the entrance to general merchandise stores, restaurants, herb shops, and tailor shops.

Many of the products sold in Chinatown's stores were imported from China. These products allowed immigrants to keep their traditions in cooking and dressing. They also attracted many non-Chinese customers who could buy fine Chinese porcelain and silk.

It was in these stores where many newcomers found their first jobs. When Ah Lung first arrived in the United States, he found a job at a Chinese store in San Francisco. This allowed him to save the funds he needed to lease land.

Growth of Chinatowns As their neighborhoods grew, the Chinese formed organizations, just as they had in the farm areas. Among the organizations that formed in the cities were **fongs.** A *fong* was made up of various families, organized to help each other in different ways. One way was by helping new arrivals. These family organizations also formed clubhouses which members used as social centers.

As Chinese farmers left rural areas in the late 1800s, they found protection in the Chinatowns. One resident of San Francisco's Chinatown said:

> Most of us can live a warmer, freer, and a more humane life among our relatives and friends than among strangers.

Although Chinese Americans were not free from anti-Chinese hostility, they could protect themselves better in

Chinatowns. The large Chinatowns offered jobs at a time when many Chinese Americans were being forced out of jobs because of prejudice.

The Chinatowns became strongholds of Chinese culture. They developed as important trading centers. The Chinese had started out in the United States as fishers, miners, gold panners, and railroad builders. By the 1900s, however, most Chinese were city dwellers. In the 1900s, Chinese culture in the United States became mostly an urban culture.

Thinking It Over

1. What were some of the laws that were passed against Chinese Americans?
2. What did the Chinese do to help each other?

CHAPTER 11 REVIEW

I. REVIEWING VOCABULARY

Match each word on the left with the correct definition on the right.

1. tenant farmer
2. *yuen*
3. *fong*

a. someone who rents land and pays rent with a portion of the crops

b. a cooperative farm company

c. an organization formed by Chinese families in the United States

II. UNDERSTANDING THE CHAPTER

1. What role did Chinese play in the California Gold Rush?
2. How were Chinese workers on the transcontinental railroad discriminated against?
3. Why did Chinese farmers become tenent farmers?
4. How did Ah Lung become the Potato King?

III. APPLYING YOUR SKILLS

Analyzing a Quotation In 1876, a representative of Chinese immigrants complained before Congress about working conditions:

Many Chinese workers expected to come here for one or two years and make a little fortune and return. But few have returned to China. Why is this? Because few among them ever thought of all these difficulties. Expensive rents, expensive living. A day without work means a day without food. For this reason, they are compelled to labor and live in poverty, quite unable to return to their native land.

List facts from this chapter that would support the speaker's point of view.

IV. WRITING ABOUT HISTORY

1. **What Would You Have Done?** Suppose you worked for a U.S. company that wanted to attract Chinese workers. Write an announcement that encourages workers to come to the United States, but also warns them of the difficulties they may face.
2. **Past to Present** Suppose you are an employee of a company today that wants to attract workers from Asia to the United States. Write an honest announcement that encourages workers to come to the United States, but describes some of the difficulties they may face.

V. WORKING TOGETHER

With other classmates, prepare a bulletin board display about the contributions of Chinese immigrants to the U.S. in the 1800's.

CHAPTER 12
CLARA BARTON: ANGEL OF THE BATTLEFIELD

PEOPLE, PLACES, AND EVENTS

Antietam

U.S. Sanitary Commission

Geneva Treaty

Red Cross

VOCABULARY

civil service

veteran

MULTICULTURAL MILESTONES

- Clara Barton challenged accepted limits by doing work previously done only by males.
- Barton was one of a number of women who made important contributions during the Civil War.
- Barton founded the American Red Cross.

Defying the generals, a short, dark-haired woman named Clara Barton braved Confederate fire to care for wounded Union soldiers.

PATHS TO THE PRESENT: CHALLENGING THE LIMITS

In Clara Barton's day, there were very strong limits placed on the right of women to have careers. One hundred fifty years ago, few jobs outside the home were open to women. Society said to Clara Barton, "You can't do this. You can't do that." Clara Barton said to society, "Yes, I can!" And she did it.

Much has changed since Clara Barton's day. But Americans today are still challenging society's limits. What is your challenge? Do you have a goal? Few of us will be able to accomplish what Clara Barton did. All of us, however, have the power to set goals and work to achieve them.

SETTING THE STAGE: THE CIVIL WAR

The Civil War was one of the major milestones in U.S. history. Four years of struggle between the North and the South brought many changes to this nation. Life for tens of thousands of U.S. families would never be the same after sons, fathers, and husbands who fought in the war were killed or wounded.

The war had a great impact on the lives of women. Women from the North and South worked hard to support soldiers fighting in the field. Women labored in factories and on farms, raised money for supplies, and cared for the sick and wounded. They showed that women were able organizers and workers.

The story of Clara Barton shows how the Civil War affected the life of one woman. Clara Barton became the best-known woman to be involved in the Civil War. But she was far from alone.

Some women, like Barton, worked to provide better care for soldiers. Elizabeth Blackwell, the first woman doctor in the United States, was a founder of the U.S. Sanitary Commission. This organization worked to improve the health and safety of Union troops.

Before the war, Dorothea Dix had become famous for her efforts to improve the care of the mentally ill. When fighting began, Dix urged that a unit of women nurses be formed. At first, Dix found little support. She pushed on anyway and finally won approval.

African American women also served as nurses. Harriet Tubman was famous for helping African Americans escape from slavery. During the Civil War, she served as head nurse at a hospital for African Americans in Virginia. Sojourner Truth, the abolitionist and fighter for women's rights, also volunteered as a nurse.

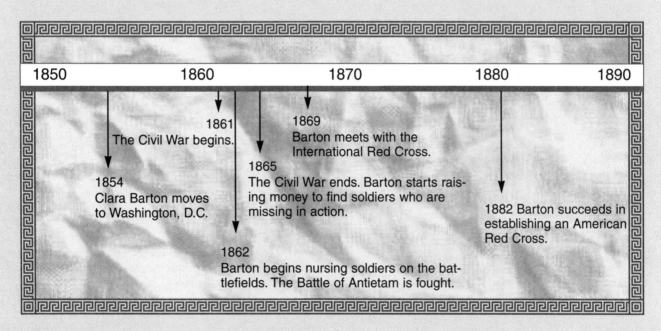

| 1850 | 1860 | 1870 | 1880 | 1890 |

1861
The Civil War begins.

1869
Barton meets with the International Red Cross.

1854
Clara Barton moves to Washington, D.C.

1865
The Civil War ends. Barton starts raising money to find soldiers who are missing in action.

1882 Barton succeeds in establishing an American Red Cross.

1862
Barton begins nursing soldiers on the battlefields. The Battle of Antietam is fought.

It was the fall of 1862. The Civil War had been raging for more than a year. In September, Confederate troops marched to the banks of Antietam (an-TEET-uhm) Creek in Maryland. There, they faced the Union army in what was to become the bloodiest day in U.S. history.

The fighting began at dawn on September 17. It ended at sunset. In those few hours, more than 12,000 Union troops fell dead or wounded. Confederate losses were smaller—just over 10,000. A woman who lived nearby described the shocking scene:

> The wounded filled every building and overflowed into the country round, into farm-houses, barns, corn-cribs, cabins—wherever four walls and a roof were found together.

Even as the battle raged, efforts to aid the wounded went on. For many of the fallen soldiers, aid came in the form of a short, dark-haired woman wearing a black dress with its hem pinned up to her waist. Her name was Clara Barton.

SECTION 1: CLARA BARTON BECOMES A TEACHER.

Barton reached Antietam shortly after the first guns began to fire. She took charge of some soldiers and led them onto the battlefield in search of the wounded. She bandaged the wounds of injured soldiers and gave them words of hope. She brought water to these soldiers. Many were too weak to sit up to drink it. She reported that once, as she held a soldier up, "a bullet sped its way between us, tearing a hole in my sleeve and found its way into his body."

Angel of the Battlefield Barton aided doctors as they amputated mangled arms and legs. She even performed an emergency operation herself. Responding to a young soldier's cries of pain, she removed a bullet from his face using her pocketknife.

No one who saw them would ever forget the scenes of devastation on the battlefields. Here, at Antietam in 1862, bodies lay rotting in the fields for weeks after the battle.

CLARA BARTON: ANGEL OF THE BATTLEFIELD

For days, Barton brought help and hope to the wounded. The soldiers she aided and the doctors she assisted remembered her. The soldiers gave her the name "the angel of the battlefield."

Early Days No one would have guessed that Clara Barton would one day be thought of as an "angel of the battlefield." Barton was born in 1821 in the town of North Oxford, Massachusetts. Barton's mother, Sarah, was an independent-minded woman. She signed some of the first antislavery petitions sent to the U.S. Congress. She also believed strongly in women's rights. She passed this belief on to Clara.

The Barton family owned a small farm and a sawmill in North Oxford. They were not rich, but comfortably middle class. In the early 1800s, women from such families were expected to marry and raise families. Professional careers for these women were rare. They might take jobs as factory workers, or maids. Due to the work of Catherine Beecher (see Chapter 7), women were also now free to take work as teachers. But such jobs were thought of as temporary, something to do until they married.

A Teaching Career Clara Barton became a school teacher. At age 18, she taught her first class in a one-room schoolhouse in North Oxford. With her skill and ability, she began to think of teaching as a lifelong career.

Soon, Barton was in demand as a teacher in many nearby schools. At the time, it was common to pay women teachers less than men. Clara refused to go along with this system. She told one school board, "I may sometimes be willing to teach for nothing. But if you pay me at all, I shall never do a man's work for less than a man's pay."

Barton moved to New Jersey in 1851. Unlike Massachusetts, New Jersey at that time had only a handful of public schools. The town of Bordentown, New Jersey, had none. Barton began an effort to bring public education to the children of Bordentown.

Barton's effort taught her how to work within the town's political system to achieve her goal. First, she became friendly with a member of the local school board and won him over to her cause. Then, he arranged for Barton to speak to the full school board. Her clear arguments convinced the board. It gave its approval for a public school.

But Barton's job was not done. The people of Bordentown feared that free education must be bad education. When the Bordentown school opened in July 1852, Barton had no pupils.

Barton was not discouraged. She spoke to children who passed by the school yard. Her pleasant manner stirred the children's interest. By day's end, she had six pupils. By the end of the week, she had nearly 40. By the end of the term, the schoolhouse was overflowing. In the following years, Bordentown built a new schoolhouse with eight classrooms that would hold all of the town's 600 students.

Barton's career as a teacher continued for almost 15 years. During that time, she was respected as a popular teacher and as a supporter of public education. Finally, she decided that she wanted something new.

Working for the Government Clara Barton moved to Washington, D.C., and began a new career. In July 1854, she began work as clerk in the U.S. Patent Office.

Barton was one of the first women to hold a job in the U.S. **civil service.** The civil service includes all government jobs,

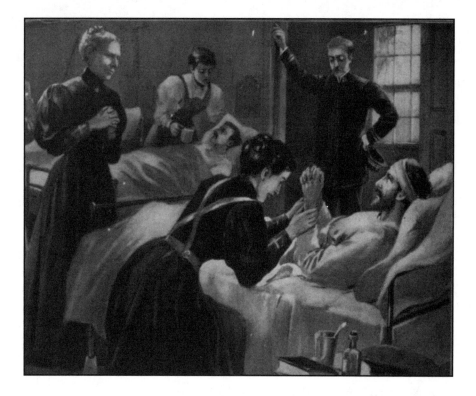

Later in her life, when there were wounded to help, Barton did not shirk her duty. During the Cuban-Spanish-American war, she aided wounded American soldiers in Havana, Cuba.

except for elected positions or those in the military. Barton did her job well. But she had to struggle against the hostility of male workers. At times, male clerks jeered at her. They lined the halls as she walked by, blowing cigar smoke in her face and spitting tobacco juice at her skirts. Despite these insults, Barton worked at the Patent Office for three years.

War Begins After a brief stay at North Oxford, she returned to the Patent Office in Washington in 1860. By that time, Washington was the capital of a dividing nation. After Abraham Lincoln was elected President, some southern states seceded, or withdrew from, the United States. In 1861, the Civil War began.

Washington, D.C., stood on the border of the Confederacy. Trains frequently brought wounded soldiers to the city. Barton started meeting the trains. She arranged for some of the most severely wounded soldiers to be taken to hospitals. Then, she visited stores, convincing owners to send food to the hungry soldiers. Barton visited with the wounded soldiers, reading newspapers and comforting them.

In the first days of the Civil War, Clara Barton had found work that would give her the sense of purpose she needed. Barton would do all in her power to care for "her boys," as she thought of the Union troops. "So far as our poor efforts can reach, they shall never lack a kindly hand or a sister's sympathy if they come," she wrote.

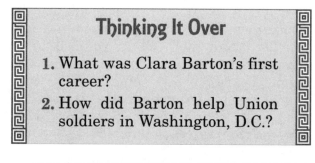

Thinking It Over

1. What was Clara Barton's first career?
2. How did Barton help Union soldiers in Washington, D.C.?

SECTION 2:
CLARA BARTON BEGINS A
NEW MISSION.

Barton now dedicated herself to her new mission. The Union army was short of supplies needed to feed and treat the soldiers. Barton visited hospitals and camps to distribute tobacco, soap, and lemons to the troops.

Collecting Supplies Barton realized that more goods were needed. She wrote letters to newspapers, asking people to send supplies to her. In a short time, she had collected three warehouses full of goods.

The Union soldiers were grateful for Barton's visits. But she felt she had to do still more. In the summer of 1861, the Union army suffered major defeats in Virginia. The wounded soldiers flooded the hospitals and camps around Washington. The suffering of the soldiers deeply moved Barton. She wanted to get to the battlefields, to bring soldiers aid as quickly as possible. This would be her new mission, to bring medical care to the wounded "anywhere between the bullet and the hospital."

Yet Barton hesitated. At that time, most people believed that "respectable" women had no place near army camps or battlefield hospitals. Nursing was not an "acceptable" career for women.

Still uncertain what to do, Barton went back to Massachusetts to visit her dying father. He told her that a respectable woman would always be treated with respect, even on battlefields and in field hospitals. He urged her to "serve my country with all I had, even my life if need be." After his death, she returned to Washington with no doubts.

On the Battlefield Barton still had to convince army officials to accept her aid. It was one thing for women to collect supplies. It was quite another for them to look after wounded soldiers while cannon balls and rifle bullets filled the air.

At first, army officers ignored Barton's requests for passes to the front lines. But she continued to ask them. Finally, she got a pass to the main camp of the Union army in Virginia.

The pass was supposed to be good for one trip only to the main camp. But when Barton got word of a battle in August

Clara Barton made nursing a "respectable" profession for women. Nursing became one of the best-paying careers for 19th century women.

1862, she reused the pass to reach the battlefield.

The battle was over when she reached the site, but the sight of the dead and wounded shocked her. For two days and nights, she washed and dressed wounds, made bandages, cooked for and fed the wounded. Barton returned to Washington exhausted. However, she was sure that she was doing the right thing.

Barton knew that getting aid to the field as soon as possible was vital. "I did not wait for reporters and journalists to tell us that a battle had been fought," she said. "I went in while the battle raged." She rushed to other battlefields. She brought food, comfort, and care to thousands of the wounded in the harshest conditions. Once, she wrote, "The weight of the blood soaking my clothing was so great I could hardly walk. I had to wring the blood from the bottom of my clothing before I could step.

But Barton did more than care for the soldiers. She prodded army and government officials to improve medical care. She pushed for a new ambulance service to get the wounded to medical care more rapidly.

War's End By 1864, the efforts of Clara Barton and others to make the U.S. army's medical services more efficient were paying off. The collection and distribution of medical supplies was better organized. Larger numbers of better trained medical staff traveled with the army and worked in its hospitals.

The end of the war did not mark the end of Clara Barton's efforts for "her boys." Thousands of soldiers were missing in action. Many of these were buried in unmarked graves. Barton set about trying to track down information about these missing men to pass on to their families. Working with little money, Barton accounted for 22,000 of the missing.

A National Figure The Civil War had forever changed Clara Barton's life. Barton was now a public figure. Even though she felt uneasy in this role, she was willing to use her fame to achieve her goals.

Barton needed money for her work of finding missing soldiers. To help raise it, she set out on a series of lecture tours. From 1866 to 1868, she gave over 300 speeches all across the country. In them, she described her experiences in the war. To the soldiers she had helped on the battlefield, Barton was already an "angel." Now, as **veterans** flocked to her lectures, she became a national hero.

In 1868, Barton visited Europe for a rest. In Switzerland in 1869, a group of business people called on her. That meeting introduced Barton to a cause that would occupy most of the rest of her life.

The International Red Cross The business people represented the International Committee of the Red Cross. The organization had been formed in 1863 to help provide care for soldiers wounded in war. By the time of Barton's visit, 32 nations had signed what was called the Geneva Treaty. Under its terms, the wounded and prisoners of war would be protected. The United States, however, refused to sign the treaty. The business people had come to ask Clara Barton to try and persuade the U.S. government to change its mind.

Barton saw first-hand what the Red Cross could do. While she was in Europe, a war broke out between France and Germany. She worked with the International Red Cross in bringing relief

Barton never stopped devoting her life to service. Near the end of her life, she became head of the U.S. Red Cross.

to the victims of war. Barton's work in this war was not on the battlefields. Instead, she worked in cities, bringing aid to women and children displaced by war.

Gathering Support After her return home, Barton dedicated herself to bringing the Red Cross to the United States. In doing so, she faced major challenges. Women still did not have the vote. U.S. politicians therefore were not greatly interested in issues brought to them by women. After all, women could not vote them out of office.

In addition, the U.S. government still refused to sign the Geneva Treaty.

Government officials did not want to become involved in European affairs.

Barton was determined to succeed. She set out to gather support for the Red Cross. To do so, she wrote pamphlets and magazine articles. She traveled the country giving speeches. Women might not be able to vote, but Civil War veterans could. Barton wrote to and spoke to veterans' groups. She called on them to support her dream.

To win more public support for the Red Cross, Barton developed a new idea. The International Red Cross had chiefly focused on giving aid during war time. Now, Barton began to stress how useful the Red Cross could be in times of other disasters such as fires, floods, and outbreaks of disease.

Slowly, Barton gained support for her cause. The work took years, but she persisted. Finally, in 1882, President Chester A. Arthur signed the Geneva Treaty and the Senate approved it. Barton wrote in her diary:

> So it was done at last and I had waited so long and got so weak and broken I could not even feel glad. I laid down the letter and wiped my tired head and eyes.

Two years later, Barton went back to Europe to an International Red Cross conference. This time, she went as a representative of the American Red Cross. As the conference ended, a delegate from Europe rose to speak. He offered Clara Barton the thanks of all the people of the world for bringing the United States into the Red Cross. As he did, the conference members rose and cheered her name.

Later Years Barton headed the U.S. Red Cross from its founding till 1904. During that time, the organization brought aid to victims of floods on the

Ohio River; of a dam collapse in Johnstown, Pennsylvania; and of a yellow fever epidemic in Florida. She helped make the Red Cross a respected symbol in the United States.

After her retirement, Barton spoke forcefully in favor of equal pay for women and for their right to vote. Barton died in 1912 at the age of 91. She was buried in her childhood home of North Oxford, Massachusetts.

Thinking It Over

1. How did Barton help the families of soldiers after the Civil War?
2. Why did the U.S. government not want to sign the Geneva Treaty?

CHAPTER 12 REVIEW

I. REVIEWING VOCABULARY

Match each word on the left with the correct definition on the right.

1. veteran
2. secede
3. civil service

a. to withdraw from the union
b. term used to describe all government jobs, except for elected positions
c. a person who has served in the military

II. UNDERSTANDING THE CHAPTER

1. What contribution did Clara Barton make to public education in the state of New Jersey?
2. What difficulties did Barton face in her job as a U.S. government clerk?
3. How did Barton aid Union soldiers during the Civil War?
4. What were some of the roles women played during the Civil War?
5. How did Barton use her relationship with Civil War veterans to gain support for the Red Cross?

III. APPLYING YOUR SKILLS

Drawing Conclusions A conclusion is a statement supported by facts. Read the following statement, then list any facts that you can find in the chapter to support it: "Clara Barton was willing to challenge the commonly accepted limits on women's roles in U.S. life."

IV. WRITING ABOUT HISTORY

1. **What Would You Have Done?** You are a Union general during the Civil War. Clara Barton comes to you with a request to help the wounded on the battlefield. You fear that if she is herself wounded or killed, you will face severe criticism. Write a brief statement telling whether or not you will allow Barton to assist on the battlefield.

2. **Past to Present** A statue of Clara Barton is about to be dedicated in her hometown of North Oxford, Massachusetts. You have been asked to give a short speech on the topic: "Clara Barton's effect on people today." Write out your speech and present it to the class.

V. WORKING TOGETHER

With a group of classmates, draw a poster that highlights the achievements of women during the Civil War. Display your poster in your classroom.

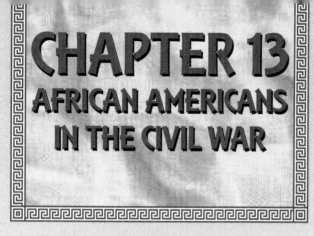

CHAPTER 13
AFRICAN AMERICANS IN THE CIVIL WAR

PEOPLE, PLACES, AND EVENTS

Frederick Douglass
Port Hudson
Milliken's Bend
Fort Wagner

VOCABULARY

border states
contraband
emancipation

MULTICULTURAL MILESTONES

- President Abraham Lincoln issued the Emancipation Proclamation.
- African Americans were accepted into the Union army.
- African American troops were given the opportunity to fight.

African American troops, such as these two at Port Hudson in 1863, fought with valor to help preserve the Union.

PATHS TO THE PRESENT: FIGHTING RACISM

The dictionary defines racism as "the belief that some races, or groups of people, are by nature superior to others." Most people today know that racism is wrong. No one group of people is superior to another. People should be valued for their individual abilities.

During the Civil War, many whites held the racist belief that African Americans would not make good soldiers. However, when African American troops were formed, they proved the racists wrong. African American troops fought bravely.

All of us must look for ways to end racist beliefs and actions. The best place to begin is within ourselves. Then we must work to change the thoughts and feelings of those around us.

SETTING THE STAGE: BATTLING SLAVERY

At the beginning of the Civil War, President Abraham Lincoln made it clear that his main goal was to restore the Union. It was not to end slavery. Lincoln once said, "If I could save the Union without freeing any slave I would do it, and if I could save it by freeing all the slaves I would do it; and if I could save it by freeing some and leaving others alone I would also do that."

But the issue of slavery had been a main cause of the war. The question of what to do about enslaved African Americans could not be avoided. African Americans themselves, both free and enslaved, would not permit that to happen. They urged President Lincoln and other politicians in the North to use the war to put a final end to slavery. They did more than talk. They showed themselves ready to work and to fight for an end to slavery.

At first, few considered the offers of African Americans to aid in the struggle. Many people opposed African Americans in the armed forces due to prejudice. As the war went on, though, and the Union suffered through many defeats, the idea of letting African Americans join in the fighting won acceptance.

Despite discrimination in the army, thousands of African Americans rushed to join the effort. This chapter tells how African Americans came to play a major part in what became a war both to restore the Union and to end slavery.

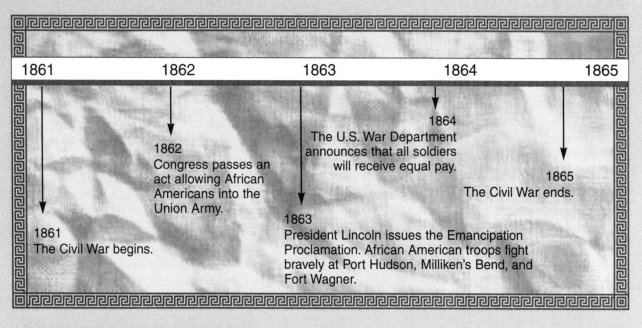

1861   1862   1863   1864   1865

1864
The U.S. War Department announces that all soldiers will receive equal pay.

1862
Congress passes an act allowing African Americans into the Union Army.

1865
The Civil War ends.

1861
The Civil War begins.

1863
President Lincoln issues the Emancipation Proclamation. African American troops fight bravely at Port Hudson, Milliken's Bend, and Fort Wagner.

In the early morning hours of April 12, 1861, the roar of cannons shattered the air of the harbor at Charleston, South Carolina. Confederate guns had opened fire on Fort Sumter, an island in the harbor. That fort was held by Union troops. The firing on the fort marked the beginning of the Civil War.

One person who feared the struggle might turn into a long one was Frederick Douglass. Douglass was an African American who had escaped from slavery in the South. He had since become one of the leading abolitionists in the North. Just weeks after Fort Sumter, Douglass set out his plan to ensure a quick end to the war.

In his magazine *Douglass' Monthly*, he demanded that African Americans take part in the fighting. He said the U.S. government should

> let the slaves and free colored people be called into service, and formed into a liberating army. Let us march into the South and raise the banner of freedom among the slaves.

The Union Army was slow to use African Americans in combat. At first, they were used to build roads and guard supplies.

SECTION 1:
AFRICAN AMERICANS JOIN THE STRUGGLE.

Few people in the North at that time agreed with Douglass. President Abraham Lincoln was not one of them.

As you have read, Lincoln's goal was to put the Union back together. If he were to do this, he would have to keep all the states that had sided with the North in the Union. But four of those states—Missouri, Kentucky, Maryland, and Delaware—were slave states. They were known as **border states.**

Lincoln feared that if he allowed African Americans to fight in the army or called for an end to slavery, he might anger the border states. They might then secede and join the Confederacy.

In the South Strangely enough, the Confederate states were the first to use African Americans in their armies. They were used as laborers. Soldiers in those days had to do much heavy labor. Trenches had to be dug. Forts had to be built. Supply wagons had to be loaded and driven.

White Southerners thought that African Americans in their army would free up white soldiers for fighting. In fact, most African Americans who joined did so as laborers. But some African Americans did fight with Confederate troops.

Confederate use of African Americans as fighters remained low, however. White

Even as the war went against the Union, Northern officers used African Americans as servants, rather than as fighters. African Americans had to win the right to be combat soldiers.

Southerners in general did not want to put weapons into the hands of African Americans. They feared a general uprising of slaves might break out. Only at the very end of the war, when they desperately needed soldiers did the Confederate government call for the enlistment of enslaved African Americans.

Runaway Slaves The use of African Americans in the Confederate army put pressure on Lincoln to change the policies of the Union. Other pressure came from the African Americans of the South.

As soon as Union armies began to march into the South, enslaved African Americans began to flee toward those armies. Lincoln may have claimed he was not fighting to free the slaves. However, the slaves themselves felt differently. Thousands risked their lives to travel to Union lines.

At first, the Union army had no set policy toward these runaways. Some generals even sent them back to their Southern owners. Other generals, however, refused to do so. Some felt slavery was evil and that it was wrong to send runaways back to it. Others felt that the runaways

deprived the South of valuable labor and thus hurt its chances in the war.

One such Union general was Benjamin Butler who commanded forces in Virginia. When a southern slave owner asked for return of some runaway slaves, Butler replied that Virginia was now "a foreign country." He did not have to return runaway slaves. Butler said the runaways were "contraband of war." This meant they were property of one country that an enemy has the right to seize during a war. Soon, the Union began calling runaway African American slaves **contraband.**

Butler put the escaped slaves to work around his camp. Soon, other Union generals began to follow Butler's lead.

In many cases, African Americans were doing labor similar to what they had done on southern plantations. But now they were being paid for their work. During the war, about half a million African Americans fled to Union troops. About 200,000 of these went to work for the army.

Emancipation As the war dragged on into 1862, things looked bleak for the Union army. The Confederate army

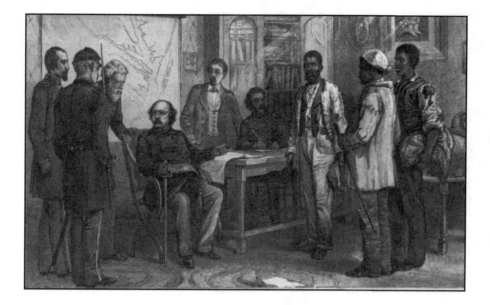

General Benjamin Butler, seated at left, treated runaway slaves as property seized during a war. Escaped slaves were put to work around the Union camp.

under Robert E. Lee had won several major battles. Lincoln was beginning to share the view of generals like Butler that freeing slaves would weaken the Confederate cause. Frederick Douglass explained it best:

> The very stomach of this rebellion is the use of slave labor. End this, and you smite [hit] the rebellion in the very seat of its life.

By September, Lincoln announced that on January 1, 1863, he would issue an order calling for the **emancipation,** or freeing, of slaves. This Emancipation Proclamation would free slaves in those areas still in revolt against the United States. It would not free slaves in the border states or in areas already held by Union troops.

Enlistment Lincoln had not rushed to issue his Emancipation Proclamation. Nor did he rush to let African Americans into the army. Again, he used the border states as an excuse not to act.

Other Northerners did not want African Americans in the army for other reasons. Some feared that arming African Americans would set off a bloody uprising. Others were prejudiced. They felt that only whites should wear the uniform of the Union army. They claimed that African Americans would not make good soldiers.

But pressure from army leaders to use African Americans mounted. As the Union suffered defeat after defeat, Congress changed its mind. In July 1862, Congress passed an act allowing the use of "persons of African descent." The act said such troops would be paid $10 a month, $3 of which might be part of their clothing expenses. White troops got $13 a month plus clothing expenses.

Despite the unequal pay rates, African Americans began to join up. Soon, regiments of African American soldiers were formed in Louisiana, South Carolina, and Kansas. All these regiments were led by white officers.

African Americans were now in the Union army. For many people, however the question remained: How would they fight?

AFRICAN AMERICANS IN THE CIVIL WAR

At Fort Wagner, South Carolina, the 54th Massachusetts Regiment charged the walls under deadly fire and held the fort for three hours. About 40 percent of the regiment was either killed or wounded.

Thinking It Over

1. What was President Lincoln's chief goal during the Civil War?
2. How did pay for African American soldiers differ from that of white soldiers?

SECTION 2:
AFRICAN AMERICANS GET A CHANCE TO FIGHT.

African Americans had fought for the chance to join the Union army. Once in it, they had to fight for the chance to be soldiers.

Many Union officers wanted to use the new units of African American troops as the laborers, just as the Confederates had done. They thought this would free up white soldiers for fighting.

But African Americans had not joined up just to use shovels. They wanted to use rifles as well. They protested to their officers. Those officers pushed their superiors to give African Americans a chance to fight.

Slowly, those chances began to come. In October 1862, African Americans from a Kansas regiment clashed with Confederates in Missouri. In March 1863, African Americans from South Carolina took part in an invasion of Florida. The African Americans handled themselves well. But these were small fights. Union officers still questioned how those troops would handle themselves in large battles.

The answer came in three bloody battles in mid-1863. In those battles, African American soldiers showed how valuable they could be to the Union.

Port Hudson The first of those battles came in May at Port Hudson, Louisiana. The Confederates had built a strong fort at Port Hudson. Already, it had turned back several Union attacks.

On May 27, three African American regiments took part in a new attack. Those regiments had been formed of free African Americans living in Louisiana. They were ordered to charge the walls of the fort. From those walls Confederate cannon aimed straight at them.

A Union general later wrote, they "made six or seven charges over this ground against the enemy's works. They

Fighting with out-of-date weapons, two regiments of African American troops held off Confederate troops. Their defense helped convince Union officers of the enormous value of African American fighters to the Union cause.

were exposed to a terrible fire and were dreadfully slaughtered." Despite this fire, they reached Confederate rifle pits at the base of the fort. They held them for three hours before being driven back by heavy cannon fire. In the fight, some 20 percent of the African American soldiers involved were killed or wounded.

The bravery of those troops deeply moved Union officers. One wrote, "You have no idea how my prejudices with regard to Negro troops have been removed by the battle the other day." Word of the courage of those troops soon spread. A New York newspaper reported:

That heap of 600 corpses is a better proclamation of freedom than even President Lincoln's. A race ready to die thus was never yet kept in bondage and never can be.

Milliken's Bend Less than two weeks later, another battle took place farther up the Mississippi. General Ulysses S. Grant had left four regiments of African American troops and one of whites to hold Milliken's Bend, a key spot on the river. Meanwhile Grant's army moved on Vicksburg. The Confederates believed that if they took Milliken's Bend they could make Grant stop the attack on Vicksburg.

Most of the African Americans at Milliken's Bend were newly enlisted. Many had received less than two weeks of training. For weapons, they had out-of-date, poorly-made rifles. Some had been trained with only two days of target practice.

On the morning of June 7, some 1,500 Confederate troops charged into the 1,200 African Americans defending Milliken's Bend. One white officer called what followed "a horrible fight, the worst I was ever engaged in."

The raw troops held off the first Confederate charges. In the face of repeated attacks, the African American troops retreated. Then they reformed and held. One officer reported:

Many of the severely wounded voluntarily returned to the ranks after washing their wounds. One soldier whose jaw was severely shattered would not leave his post, until ordered by his commander.

After repeated attacks failed to break the African Americans, the Confederates retreated.

The new troops had won. But the cost of victory was high. One regiment saw 45 percent of its members killed or wounded.

As word of the battle spread, more Union officers became convinced of the value of African American fighters. Lincoln's Assistant Secretary of War claimed

> the bravery of the blacks in the battle of Milliken's Bend completely revolutionized the feelings of the army with regard to the employment of Negro troops. Prominent officers who had sneered at the idea of negroes fighting express themselves after that in favor of it.

Fort Wagner The third key battle for African Americans that summer took place far to the east. The Union army had long hoped to seize Charleston, South Carolina, where the Civil War had begun. There, they faced a system of forts that protected the city's harbor.

In July 1863, the Union army tried to seize one of those forts, Fort Wagner. If they took it, the Union could drive Confederates out of the other forts and, in time, take Charleston. The attack came on the night of July 17. At its head was the 54th Massachusetts Regiment, made up of African American volunteers. Its commander was Robert Gould Shaw, a young white colonel from Boston.

The regiment had been formed early that year. It accepted African Americans from all across the North. Frederick Douglass himself had helped recruit troops for it. Two of his sons served in it.

The regiment trained in Massachusetts. Then in late May, it sailed to South Carolina. There, the 54th had taken part in some small actions. Now, it was going to take the lead in a major attack.

It was an almost hopeless attack. Fort Wagner was on a small, sandy island. To reach it, the soldiers had to march across a flat, narrow beach. Confederate guns could fire at them the whole way. There was no place to take cover.

But the 54th almost did it. Under deadly fire, they charged the fort. Lunging with bayonets and swinging their rifles, they fought their way over the walls and into the fort. There, they held on for almost three hours.

But no Union troops came to aid them. Badly outnumbered, they had to retreat. Behind them they left Colonel Shaw, slain on the fort's walls, and some 40 percent of their fellow soldiers killed or wounded.

The attack had failed, but word of the courage of the 54th spread. As one writer put it, the

> blacks fought as other soldiers have always fought in desperate assaults. They moved the hearts and swayed the minds of the Northern people to an appreciation of the colored soldier. We came to recognize the purpose of fighting out the war until the Negro should be free.

A Vital Role At the beginning of 1862, there had been only four regiments of African American troops in the Union Army. By the end of that year, the number grew to 60. Their numbers continued to grow, and as the war went on they served on all fronts.

By war's end, some 186,000 African Americans had served in the Union army. Another 29,000 served in the navy. About 38,000 died in the war.

African American troops continued to fight against many forms of racism and discrimination. The 54th Massachusetts, for example, took no pay at all for a year rather than take less than white soldiers got. Finally, in 1864 the U.S. War Department announced all soldiers would receive equal pay.

African American troops also faced special danger in battle. Some southern troops preferred to kill African Americans rather than take them prisoner. Any African Americans taken prisoner were usually treated worse than white prisoners.

The contributions of African American soldiers, were acknowledged by many. A former U.S. Secretary of War wrote to a member of Lincoln's Cabinet:

> The stubborn valor displayed by troops of this race at Port Hudson, Milliken's Bend, and Fort Wagner has demonstrated to the President and to the country the character of the service of which they are capable. In view of their loyalty and courage, they certainly make up, at this crisis in our history, a most powerful and reliable arm of the public defense.

Thinking It Over

1. Where did African American troops turn back a Confederate attack in June 1863?

2. What Confederate position did the 54th Massachusetts Regiment attack in July 1863?

CHAPTER 13 REVIEW

I. REVIEWING VOCABULARY

Match each word on the left with the correct definition on the right.

1. border states
2. contraband
3. emancipation

a. freeing of slaves
b. property of one country that an enemy has the right to seize during a war
c. the four slave states that sided with the Union

II. UNDERSTANDING THE CHAPTER

1. Why was President Lincoln reluctant to use African Americans as soldiers in the early days of the Civil War?
2. How did the Confederate Army use African Americans during the war?
3. What was the Emancipation Proclamation?
4. Why did many Union officers change their minds about using African American troops?

III. APPLYING YOUR SKILLS

Identifying a Point of View Read the following statement:

Every consideration of justice, humanity and sound policy confirms the wisdom of calling upon black men just now to take up arms in behalf of their country.

Which of the following would have been most likely to make that statement in early 1861? **a.** President Abraham Lincoln; **b.** a Confederate congressman; **c.** Frederick Douglass; **d.** a Union Army general. Explain your answer.

IV. WRITING ABOUT HISTORY

1. **What Would You Have Done?** Reread the quotation from Frederick Douglass on page 118. Write an editorial for the *Douglass' Monthly* calling for use of African American troops in the Union army.
2. **Past to Present** Imagine that your city or town is building a monument to honor the African American troops who fought in the Civil War. Write a short speech that a city official might give at the opening of the monument.

V. WORKING TOGETHER

Use your school or local library to find out more about one of the battles discussed in this chapter. Then work with a group of students to draw an illustrated map of the battle showing the movements of troops during the fight. Display completed maps on the bulletin board.

CHAPTER 14

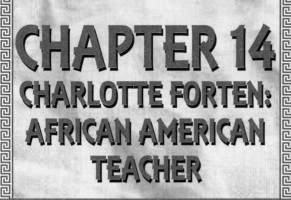

CHARLOTTE FORTEN: AFRICAN AMERICAN TEACHER

PEOPLE, PLACES, AND EVENTS

Sea Islands
Robert Smalls
Reconstruction

VOCABULARY

dialect
Gullah
freedmen

MULTICULTURAL MILESTONES

- The Union army drove Confederates from the Sea Islands, South Carolina.
- Charlotte Forten decided to teach freedmen on the Sea Islands.
- The Civil War ended and Reconstruction began.

Charlotte Forten moved into an environment like this in the Sea Islands. This photo from 1862 shows slaves preparing cotton for market.

PATHS TO THE PRESENT: VALUING AN EDUCATION

How many times have you heard someone ask you if you appreciated the education you are getting? Getting an education is easy to take for granted. Today, everyone in the United States is entitled to a free education through high school. But this was not always so.

Before the Civil War, it was nearly impossible for enslaved African Americans to get an education. In many places it was forbidden to teach enslaved African Americans to read and write. It was forbidden because slave owners realized the power of education.

During and after the Civil War, teachers like Charlotte Forten came to teach the newly freed slaves. Both the freedmen and their teachers knew that without an education enslaved African Americans would never truly be free.

SETTING THE STAGE: THE CIVIL WAR AND AFTER

Even as the Civil War raged, Union leaders worried about the future of the United States. How should they reunite the nation once the war had ended? One of the key questions was how to deal with the 4 million slaves of the South. Would they be free? If so, would they gain the right to vote? Would they have their own land? Would they be independent of their former masters? All these questions and more would need to be answered.

Education was one of the keys to advancement for African Americans in the South. Before the Civil War, southern states had made it a crime to teach enslaved African Americans to read or write. However, some free African Americans in the North had obtained good educations. They were eager to pass on their skills to the less fortunate.

During the war, Union soldiers seized control of the Sea Islands off the coast of South Carolina. Some 10,000 African Americans on the islands suddenly found themselves free. Abolitionists, or people who opposed slavery, from the North sent teachers to the South. These teachers taught the freed slaves to read and write.

Charlotte Forten was one of the first of these Northerners to head South. She was a young African American woman whose family had been free for four generations. As a member of a wealthy African American family, Forten had received a good education. She was quite excited to share her education with the people of the Sea Islands. This chapter is the story of her experiences with those people.

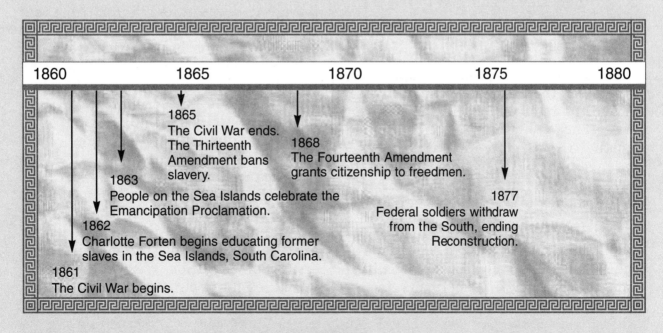

| 1860 | 1865 | 1870 | 1875 | 1880 |

1865
The Civil War ends. The Thirteenth Amendment bans slavery.

1868
The Fourteenth Amendment grants citizenship to freedmen.

1863
People on the Sea Islands celebrate the Emancipation Proclamation.

1877
Federal soldiers withdraw from the South, ending Reconstruction.

1862
Charlotte Forten begins educating former slaves in the Sea Islands, South Carolina.

1861
The Civil War begins.

As her ship made its way from New York to South Carolina's Sea Islands, 25-year-old Charlotte Forten looked from her cabin window. In the distance, she could make out the masts of ships. They were Union ships, blockading the harbor of Charleston, South Carolina. It was October 1862, and the outcome of the Civil War was still very much in doubt.

Forten shuddered. She was headed into the war zone to teach former slaves on the island of St. Helena. As an African American, she was risking her own freedom in undertaking this mission. If Confederate soldiers should take back the Sea Islands, they would grab every African American person they could find.

SECTION 1:
CHARLOTTE FORTEN TEACHES IN THE WAR ZONE.

Almost a year had passed since the fateful battle that freed the Sea Island African Americans. Union forces had driven the Confederates off the islands in November 1861. Southern planters abandoned their slaves and fled to the mainland.

With the masters gone, the African Americans laid down their tools. They broke up the cotton gins that had been a symbol of their slavery. But soon they picked the tools up, rebuilt the gins, and went back to work—as free people. Northern superintendents took over management of the plantations. The workers received wages. Many began saving money to buy land of their own.

Gullah Culture African Americans on the Sea Islands had a different culture from other African Americans in the United States. Choppy ocean waters separated the islands from the mainland. The waters had kept the island people isolated. They spoke a unique **dialect,** or regional language. It was called **Gullah.** The Gullah dialect blended West African languages with an old form of English. (It is still spoken today by some people in the Sea Islands.)

Sea Island African Americans had a well-developed culture. Many of their songs and dances came from West Africa, where their ancestors lived. Charlotte Forten and other newcomers were amazed at the songs and customs of the people.

Shortly after Forten landed in the islands, she boarded a rowboat heading for the place where she would teach school. African American rowers sang as they rowed. As the sun dropped into the sea, Forten listened to the "sweet and strange and solemn" singing of the crew. She was charmed by a hymn, which ended with the words, "No man can hinder me." It seemed a fitting statement for the newly-freed rowers to make.

Forten's Background Forten's own background was quite different from that of the Sea Island African Americans. For four generations back, neither she nor any member of her family had been subjected to slavery. Forten's family was more than free—they held an important position in African American life.

Her grandfather, James Forten Sr., had fought against the British in the American Revolution. Afterward, he became a Philadelphia sailmaker. James Forten invented a device for handling sails, and made a fortune. He used part of his wealth to support the movement for abolition. Abolition was a movement which sought to put an immediate end to slavery.

CHARLOTTE FORTEN: AFRICAN AMERICAN TEACHER

The crusade for abolition was part of Charlotte's life from the very first. Her father, James Forten Jr., was an active Philadelphia abolitionist. So were some of her aunts and uncles. Growing up, Charlotte met many leaders of the abolition movement.

Philadelphia had the largest free African American population of any American city. Yet Charlotte found the place oppressive. Whites there showed open contempt for African Americans. The public schools for African Americans were shabby and inadequate. The Forten family hired tutors to teach Charlotte at home.

Becoming a Teacher In 1853, when she was 16, Forten went to live with friends in Massachusetts. She graduated with honors from an integrated grammar school in Salem. Then she earned a teaching degree. She became the first African American teacher in Salem.

Forten submitted poems to *The Liberator,* an abolitionist newspaper, and was delighted to have them published. She hoped to become a writer. During her years in Salem, Forten started a diary in which she recorded her thoughts and activities. Thanks to this diary, we know quite a bit about her life during the Civil War years.

Helping the Freedmen In the North, antislavery groups were seeking recruits to teach the **freedmen,** as freed slaves of both sexes were called. They started the "Port Royal Experiment" (named after one of South Carolina's Sea Islands). The "experiment" aimed to show how education could turn former slaves into independent citizens.

Forten signed up with the Port Royal Relief Association. She and other teachers began arriving in the Sea Islands soon after the Union gained control.

Her first days on the Sea Islands convinced her that the experiment would work. Forten admired the eagerness of the children to learn. Older children often worked all morning in the fields, then spent all afternoon at their lessons.

Many adults came for instruction too. Forten wrote:

One old woman, who had a large family of children and grandchildren, came regularly to school in the

Forten had joined the Port Royal experiment aimed at showing how education could turn former slaves into independent citizens. What does this picture tell you about the students' desire to learn?

CHARLOTTE FORTEN: AFRICAN AMERICAN TEACHER

winter, and took her seat among the little ones. She was at least sixty years old.

Many adults could not come during the day but wanted desperately to read and write. Forten sometimes tutored those people after dark on her porch.

Schools Everywhere Throughout the South, wherever Union forces gained control, schools for freedmen opened. By the end of the war, some 200,000 freedmen were learning to read and write.

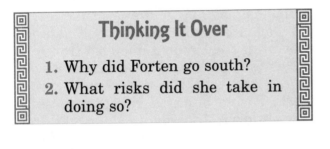

Thinking It Over

1. Why did Forten go south?
2. What risks did she take in doing so?

SECTION 2: AFRICAN AMERICANS STRUGGLE FOR EQUALITY.

The first day of January, 1863, was the most memorable day of Forten's stay in the Sea Islands. It was Emancipation Day. Forten called it "the most glorious day this nation has yet seen."

Celebrating Freedom Three months before, President Abraham Lincoln had announced a plan to emancipate, or free, all slaves in areas under Confederate control. His plan took effect January 1. Lincoln proclaimed all slaves in areas still in rebellion "then, thenceforward, and forever free."

On New Year's Day, the inhabitants of the Sea Islands, white and African American, flocked to Camp Saxton, the military base on Port Royal Island.

Bands played. Soldiers paraded. Flags flew. Solemnly, the crowd bowed its head in prayer. Later, a speaker read Lincoln's proclamation and people broke into cheers. Then came speeches. Finally, it was time for the feast. The camp's cooks had roasted 10 oxen for the occasion.

African American Regiments The soldiers stationed at Camp Saxton were almost all African Americans. They were members of the First South Carolina Volunteers. The regiment had been formed a few months earlier, mainly through the recruitment of freed Sea Island slaves. It was one of more than 100 African American regiments that fought on the Union side. (See Chapter 13.)

African American Hero From a Union officer, Forten heard of a local hero named Robert Smalls. Smalls had been a slave. He was a pilot on a Confederate ship. When the ship's officers went ashore in Charleston in 1862, Smalls and the rest of the crew ran up a Confederate flag and took the ship out to sea. They turned it over to Union forces on Port Royal Island.

As a free man, Smalls had opened a small store. He made a profit of $50 a week. But he gave that up to join the Union army, where his pay was $10 a month. Smalls said:

> How can I expect to keep my freedom if I'm not willing to fight for it? Suppose the secessionists should get back here again? What good would my fifty dollars do me then?

Land of Their Own Abolitionists believed that one of the best ways for freed slaves to advance was to have land of their own. Small farms would give them an income. They would not have to

Fleeing slaves during the Civil War expected that they would be given land and mules to start their own farms. They were to be very disappointed. Here, former slaves who escaped from the plantation of Confederate president Jefferson Davis arrive at a Union camp.

depend on their former masters for jobs. Said an African American sergeant in the Sea Islands regiment: "Every colored man will be a slave, and feel himself a slave, until he can raise his own *bale of cotton* and put his own mark upon it and say this is mine!"

But how much would the land cost? How many freed slaves would be able to afford it? The answers were: too much, and not many.

During the war, the federal government sold off most of the plantations in the Sea Islands. At a public auction in 1863, African Americans were able to buy only about 2,000 of the 16,000 acres offered. Wealthy northern whites bought the rest.

Some Americans suggested that the government should not charge freed slaves for land. It should give each family a plot of land and the equipment to farm it. "Forty acres and a mule" would help to free African Americans from their former bondage. But Congress rejected the idea. The freedmen were left to fend for themselves.

Bidding Farewell Forten's time in the Sea Islands ended before the war did. To recover from bad health, she returned to Philadelphia during the summer of 1863. She went south again in October and stayed until the following spring. Then, after receiving news of her father's death, she bid farewell to her pupils and returned to the North.

Forten's service to the freedmen did not end, however. She took a job in Boston with a freedmen's relief agency. There she helped to get aid to teachers in the South.

Reconstruction Hundreds of teachers staffed schools for the freed African Americans during Reconstruction. Reconstruction is the period from 1865 to 1877. During that time, Congress struggled to "reconstruct" the Union—to glue the North and the South back together.

For a brief time, it appeared that freed African Americans might achieve true equality. The Thirteenth Amendment (1865) banned slavery. The Fourteenth Amendment (1868) granted cititizenship to the freedmen. The Fifteenth Amendment (1870) gave free African American males the right to vote.

But equality did not come. In 1877, federal troops pulled out of the South.

Educated by Forten and others, the freedmen also wanted the same political rights as others. Here they listen to a campaign speech by an African American running for office. Political equality did not last long. In 1877, federal troops left the South and African Americans lost most of their rights.

Reconstruction ended. White southern leaders then took away many of the rights African Americans had gained. Long years passed before the barriers to African Americans began to come down.

Forten's Later Life Charlotte Forten spent the last 40 years of her life in the South. At the age of 41, she married a Presbyterian minister, Francis Grimké. Charlotte and Francis Grimké lived in Washington, D.C., and Jacksonville, Florida, where Grimké was a pastor.

Charlotte Forten Grimké continued to struggle for African American equality. In 1896, she became a founding member of the National Association of Colored Women. She died in 1914 at the age of 76.

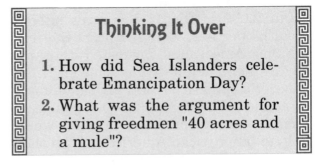

Thinking It Over

1. How did Sea Islanders celebrate Emancipation Day?
2. What was the argument for giving freedmen "40 acres and a mule"?

CHAPTER 14 REVIEW

I. REVIEWING VOCABULARY

Match each word on the left with the correct definition on the right.

1. dialect
2. Gullah
3. freedmen

a. a language spoken by African Americans of the Sea Islands
b. people who had been freed from slavery
c. a regional language

II. UNDERSTANDING THE CHAPTER

1. How did African Americans in the Sea Islands differ from African Americans elsewhere in the South?
2. Why was Charlotte Forten's family important?
3. What was the "Port Royal experiment"?
4. What advances did African Americans make during Reconstruction?
5. What happened to African Americans in the South after Reconstruction?

III. APPLYING YOUR SKILLS

Analyzing a Quotation Read the following excerpt. It is from a hymn written by John Greenleaf Whittier, at the request of Charlotte Forten. Her pupils sang it for Emancipation Day:

Oh, none in all the world before/ Were ever glad as we./ We're free on Carolina's shore;/ We're all at home and free!

Write a paragraph describing what you think the words meant to the pupils.

IV. WRITING ABOUT HISTORY

1. **What Would You Have Done?** Imagine that you were once a student in Charlotte Forten's class on St. Helena Island. Write your recollection of your feelings on the day she arrived to be your teacher. Describe what getting an education means to you.
2. **Past to Present** How has the position of African Americans in the South changed? With a small group, write a report describing changes in each of the following periods: 1862 to 1877, 1877 to 1950, and 1950 to the present.

V. WORKING TOGETHER

Choose several classmates to work with. Imagine it is 1862. Prepare an advertisement to attract teachers for freedmen's schools at a pay of $25 a month. Provide arguments that might make the job offer appealing to a northern reader.

CHAPTER 15
LILIUOKALANI: THE LAST HAWAIIAN QUEEN

Queen Liliuokalani was a Hawaiian patriot who worked to reduce American influence on the islands and restore the royal family's power.

PEOPLE, PLACES, AND EVENTS

Polynesia
Liliuokalani
David Kalakaua
Sanford B. Dole

VOCABULARY

taboo
imperialism

MULTICULTURAL MILESTONES

- Polynesian peoples settled in the Hawaiian islands.
- Europeans, Americans, and Asians began arriving in Hawaii.
- Liliuokalani lost her throne and the United States annexed Hawaii.

PATHS TO THE PRESENT: JUSTIFYING THE MEANS

Have you ever heard anyone use the expression "the ends justify the means"? What that expression means is that getting what you want is more important than worrying how you get it. Have you ever felt that way? Have you ever wanted something badly enough to do almost anything to get it?

Most people in our society believe that the ends do not justify the means. In other words, it does matter how you get what you want. How do you feel about it? As you read this chapter, think about how the U.S. government gained control of Hawaii. Think about whether the U.S. government believed that the end justifies the means. Does the U.S. government feel the same way today?

SETTING THE STAGE: END OF HAWAII'S ISOLATION

Clustered together in the waters of the north Pacific lie the Hawaiian Islands. Thousands of miles of sea separate them from the west coast of North America and the east coast of Asia. The nearest major islands in the Pacific lie far to the west and south. This region of the Pacific Ocean, from New Zealand to Hawaii, is called Polynesia. People from islands to the south settled the Hawaiian Islands by the 7th century. They became Hawaiians.

Hawaiians built a series of kingdoms, governed by rival chiefs and kings. Because of their isolated location, the Hawaiian Islands long remained cut off from the rest of the world.

Hawaii's isolation suddenly ended in 1778. A British ship commanded by Captain James Cook came upon the Hawaiian Islands while looking for a passage from the Pacific to the Atlantic. Over the century that followed, more newcomers showed up—British, French, Americans.

Outsiders upset the balance of power in Hawaii. British and other foreign ships brought guns and iron daggers. Hawaiians began trading pigs, seafood, and other products for weapons.

By 1810, one king had acquired enough weapons and ships to defeat rival kings and take over their lands. He became ruler of all 20 or so Hawaiian islands. Hawaii became a unified nation.

Soon after, missionaries and traders from the United States settled in the islands. Wealthy investors started sugar plantations. They brought people from China and Japan to do the backbreaking work. By the 1890s, native Hawaiians were a minority in their own land.

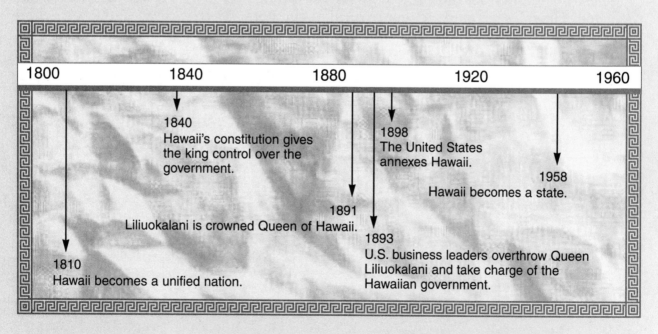

1800   1840   1880   1920   1960

1840
Hawaii's constitution gives the king control over the government.

1898
The United States annexes Hawaii.

1958
Hawaii becomes a state.

1891
Liliuokalani is crowned Queen of Hawaii.

1893
U.S. business leaders overthrow Queen Liliuokalani and take charge of the Hawaiian government.

1810
Hawaii becomes a unified nation.

On Saturday, January 14, 1893, all the majesty of Hawaiian royalty was on display. Diamonds glistened from the crown of Queen Liliuokalani (lily-uh-woe-kah-LAH-nee). A cloak draped the chair on which she sat. The Hawaiian legislature was ending its session. Precisely at noon, Liliuokalani led the closing. Her eyes gleamed with determination, a look that Hawaiians had come to expect from the proud queen.

How could anyone know that an era was drawing to a close? A chain of events was about to begin that would put an end to royal rule and thrust Hawaii onto a new course.

What events led to this turning point in Hawaii's history? Read on to find out.

SECTION 1:
HAWAII BECOMES A MULTICULTURAL SOCIETY.

By the early 1800s, Hawaii had become a popular stopover for sailors and traders who crossed the Pacific. Many of them were from the United States.

These outsiders from the United States enjoyed Hawaii's tropical climate and way of life. The outsiders would, however, bring many changes to Hawaii in the years to come.

Breaking Taboos One of the first things to change was Hawaiian's traditional religion. The traditional Hawaiian religion had many gods. It had a system of **taboos** (tah-BOOZ), or prohibitions, that helped to keep order.

After the coming of outsiders, traditional religion declined in Hawaii. Many began to break religious rules. Even Hawaii's kings began breaking the rules. The old religion was dying. But what would take its place?

Missionaries In 1820, Protestant missionaries from Boston arrived in the islands. They were eager to convert the Hawaiians to the Christian faith.

The missionaries started schools at which Hawaiians learned Christianity while learning to read and write. Up to that time the Hawaiians had not had a written language. Now Hawaiian words appeared in print.

More and more Hawaiians—including members of the royal family—became

Increasing control by foreigners made many Hawaiians long for the days less than a century before, when Hawaiian outrigger canoes roamed the seas unmolested.

Reading a Map: Which is the largest of the Hawaiian islands? On which island is Pearl Harbor located? Which is the northern-most of the Hawaiian islands.

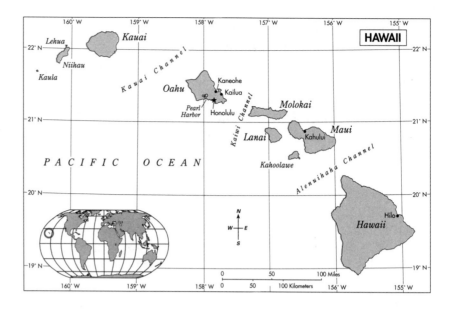

converts to the Christian faith. By 1840, about one Hawaiian in every four belonged to a Christian church.

Age of Imperialism Outside powers wanted control of Hawaii since it was first discovered. The 19th century was an age of **imperialism.** Imperialism is a policy by which one country takes control of other countries or regions. Major powers were building empires that spanned the world. Britain and France had their eyes on Hawaii—and so did the United States.

In 1842, the United States warned European powers to keep their hands off Hawaii. That did not stop Britain and France from trying to win favor with the islands' rulers.

Workers From Asia All the while, foreigners were streaming into the islands to seek their fortunes. Some of these outsiders started their own trading businesses. Some bought land on which to grow crops like sugar.

Sugar plantations needed a large supply of cheap workers. Most Hawaiians were not interested. They gained a decent income from small farms, fishing, or other jobs. Besides, the population of native Hawaiians was declining. Many Hawaiians had died of diseases brought in by outsiders.

So plantation owners looked for workers elsewhere. They shipped in workers from Asian countries—first China, later Japan. The workers came on three-year contracts. They were treated as little more than slaves. However, when their contracts ended, many Asians stayed on in Hawaii.

By the 1890s, Hawaii was a multicultural society. Hawaiians made up one third of the population. Asians made up another third. The remainder were mainly Americans and Europeans.

The Americans enjoyed influence far beyond their numbers. They owned two thirds of the property in the islands. Many served in the island's government.

Hawaii's Government Hawaii gained a written constitution in 1840. It gave the king most of the power. Only a limited group of people—mainly those with education or property—could vote.

As time went on, some Hawaiians and

outsiders began to grumble. They argued that the king was using his power as he pleased, not according to the law. In 1887, a group of Hawaiian reformers and outsiders forced King David Kalakaua to grant a new constitution. The new constitution took away most of the power of the monarch. It increased the powers of the legislature. Reformers said the new constitution made Hawaii's government more democratic.

However, many native Hawaiians disliked the new constitution. They saw it as a way for outsiders to take power. They denied that the new constitution was democratic. Voting restrictions still kept Hawaiian commoners from having much of a voice. Asians had no vote at all.

One of those who objected to the new constitution was Liliuokalani, the king's sister. She was next in line for the throne. Liliuokalani complained that the king was a weakling. *She* would show more strength.

"Queen Lil" In January 1891, King David Kalakaua died. The power passed onto Liliuokalani who was dubbed "Queen Lil" by the U.S. press. At age 52, Liliuokalani was a woman of great strength and dignity.

As queen, Liliuokalani set out to change the constitution of 1887. In January 1893, she was ready to make her move.

At the end of the official ceremonies closing the Hawaiian legislature, the queen issued an invitation. Members of the legislature were to go to her palace across the street that very afternoon. Liliuokalani did not say just what was supposed to happen. But word quickly spread that she intended to proclaim a new constitution.

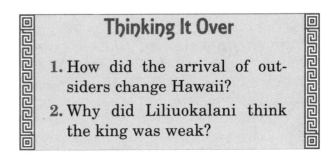

Thinking It Over

1. How did the arrival of outsiders change Hawaii?
2. Why did Liliuokalani think the king was weak?

By the middle of the 1800s, large numbers of Japanese workers had come to Hawaii to fill the growing demand for sugar plantation workers. Attracting immigrants from all of Asia, Hawaii was very much a multicultural society.

LILIUOKALANI: THE LAST HAWAIIAN QUEEN

SECTION 2:
REVOLT AND ANNEXATION CHANGE HAWAII'S HISTORY.

The queen's plan touched off a crisis. The island's business leaders were opposed to increasing the powers of the monarchy. It was time for a showdown.

The Revolution of 1893 The queen's plan to act fell through when two members of the cabinet refused to sign the new constitution. Without their signatures, the document would have no legal force. Liliuokalani was furious. But she agreed to talk about changing the document.

U.S. business leaders decided to overthrow the monarchy before the queen had time to act. They formed a "committee of safety" to organize a new government. They chose Sanford B. Dole to head the government. The conspirators also assembled a fighting force.

Advised of the plan, the U.S. ambassador sent U.S. sailors "to protect U.S. citizens." But they were clearly there to support the revolution. On January 17, the committee seized control of the government building. Its members declared an end to the monarchy. They announced the creation of a temporary government. Almost at once, the U.S. ambassador to Hawaii recognized the new government on behalf of the United States.

Liliuokalani's Reaction The queen and her supporters had been outmaneuvered. But she did not give up the fight. In the months ahead, she would struggle to persuade the U.S. people to help her get her kingdom back.

A Drive for Annexation The temporary government had quite a different idea. It asked the United States to annex Hawaii—that is, to make it part of the United States.

Annexation had a strong appeal for some Hawaiians and many outsiders. They saw annexation as a way to assure stable government for Hawaii. Stable government would help the islands' businesses to prosper.

Many white outsiders had yet another reason to want annexation. They were afraid that Hawaiians and Asians might join forces to control an independent Hawaii. However, if the United States annexed Hawaii, more whites would probably come to live there.

Political Snags Annexation of Hawaii quickly became an issue in U.S. politics. Supporters of annexation argued that it would keep Britain or France from snatching Hawaii. They also claimed that annexation would end a corrupt monarchy.

Opponents of annexation argued that U.S. support for the rebels had been a shameful power play. They said it was clearly motivated by imperialism. The United States should have consulted Hawaiians before annexation was even considered.

U.S. President Grover Cleveland sent a commissioner to Hawaii to investigate the case for annexation. The commissioner's report said most Hawaiians opposed annexation.

Cleveland seemed ready to support a return to power of Liliuokalani. But he wanted her to "forgive and forget." She bluntly refused to pardon the people who had overthrown her.

The Republic of Hawaii Since the prospects for annexation had dimmed, the new Hawaiian government made itself permanent. A new Republic of Hawaii came into being. Its constitution carefully kept power in the hands of the white minority.

Supporters of the monarchy tried to stage a revolt early in 1895. However, the republic's government clamped down hard. It put down the revolt and arrested Queen Liliuokalani. She was released only after signing a document giving up her position as queen and promising to support the new government.

Annexation: Round Two A few years later, Hawaii's leaders made a second bid for annexation. The year was 1898—the same year the United States took over the Philippines.

Supporters of a strong U.S. navy were now arguing that annexing Hawaii would make the United States a strong Pacific power. Congress decided to act. Hawaii officially became a United States territory on August 12, 1898.

Hawaii Today In 1958, Hawaii became a state. Today, resort hotels welcome tourists to the islands and modern industries employ many people.

Hawaii's multicultural traditions remain strong. Hawaii is the only state in which whites are a minority. Three people in every five are Asians or Pacific Islanders.

Whites no longer dominate Hawaiian politics. Voting rules are much like those in the rest of the United States, assuring a voice to all. In 1993, U.S. President Clinton signed a formal apology issued by Congress to the Hawaiian people. Congress apologized for the part it played in the overthrow of the Hawaiian monarchy.

Many modern Hawaiians look back upon Liliuokalani, the islands' last queen, with respect. They know her not only as a queen but also as a writer of songs. The best known of her songs is *Aloha Oe* ("Farewell to Thee"). The former queen lived on the mainland for a time, then returned to Hawaii. She died in 1917 at the age of 79.

Thinking It Over

1. What role did the United States play in the revolution of 1893?
2. What arguments were made for and against the annexation of Hawaii?

CHAPTER 15 REVIEW

I. REVIEWING VOCABULARY

Match each word on the left with the correct definition on the right.

1. taboo
2. imperialism
3. annex

a. a policy by which one country takes control of other countries or regions
b. to add a territory to an existing country
c. a prohibition

II. UNDERSTANDING THE CHAPTER

1. What changes did Protestant missionaries bring to Hawaii?
2. What major nations were interested in gaining control of Hawaii in the 1800s?
3. How did Hawaii gain a large population of Asians?
4. Why did Liliuokalani try to get a new Constitution passed?
5. What was the Revolution of 1893?

III. APPLYING YOUR SKILLS

1. **Supporting Generalizations** Write three generalizations about the role that foreigners played in bringing change to Hawaii. Give evidence from the chapter to support your generalizations.
2. **Understanding Chronology** Write a series of at least 10 newspaper headlines describing major events covered in this chapter. Arrange the headlines in the order in which the events happened.

IV. WRITING ABOUT HISTORY

1. **What Would You Have Done?** If you had been a resident of Hawaii in 1893, would you have supported or opposed annexation to the United States? Write a letter to a friend in the United States that gives arguments in support of your opinion.
2. **Past to Present** Write an article explaining how Hawaii's population became so multicultural. Include a description of how you imagine that this diversity affects Hawaii today.

V. WORKING TOGETHER

Chose two or three classmates to work with. Find pictures of ships that might have been seen in Hawaii during the 19th century. Create a model of such a ship, or draw a historical scene that shows one such ship.

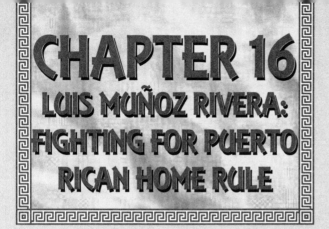

CHAPTER 16
LUIS MUÑOZ RIVERA: FIGHTING FOR PUERTO RICAN HOME RULE

In a few days of fighting U.S. troops took over Puerto Rico. In October 1898, the U.S. flag was raised over buildings in San Juan.

PEOPLE, PLACES, AND EVENTS

el Grito de Lares
Foraker Act
Jones Bill

VOCABULARY

autonomy
resident commissioner
commonwealth

MULTICULTURAL MILESTONES

- Puerto Rico was given some measure of self-rule from Spain.
- The United States took Puerto Rico from Spain and made it a U.S. colony.
- The U.S. Congress passed the Foraker Act and the Jones Act.

PATHS TO THE PRESENT: FIGHTING FOR YOUR BELIEFS

Have you ever spent time and energy to fight for a cause you believed in? Perhaps you collected signatures for a petition. Maybe you participated in a boycott. You may have even written a letter to your representative in Washington, D.C. Through whatever action you took, you were fighting for your beliefs.

Many people choose an issue and devote some time to it. The types of causes people choose might include saving the environment, preventing cruelty to animals, or stopping the spread of drugs in their neighborhood.

However, most people would not dedicate their entire life to a cause. The subject of this chapter, Luis Muñoz Rivera, dedicated his whole life to the cause of self-rule for Puerto Rico.

SETTING THE STAGE: THE SPANISH-AMERICAN WAR

In 1898, the United States declared war on Spain. The war grew out of a revolution in Cuba. Cuban revolutionaries were fighting for independence from Spain. Many Americans sympathized with the Cubans.

The Cuban-Spanish-American War lasted a few weeks. When the dust had cleared, the United States had won. It took over three Spanish possessions. The islands of Puerto Rico and Cuba in the Caribbean, and the Philippines in Southeast Asia.

For U.S. leaders, the conflict had been "a splendid little war." The United States had won a clear victory. It had acquired its first colonies, Puerto Rico and the Philippines. (After being occupied by the United States, Cuba gained independence in 1902.) The United States was now considered a world power.

For the people of Puerto Rico, though, the war was not splendid at all. They had exchanged one colonial master, Spain, for another, the United States. And the new master took back some of the rights that the old master had granted.

Puerto Ricans struggled for years to win **autonomy**, or self-rule, from Spain. Then they had to work to regain the freedoms that they had so briefly enjoyed. One man stood at the forefront of the fight for freedom. He was Luis Muñoz Rivera.

Muñoz Rivera came from a family that was involved in politics. Like most Puerto Ricans, he had strong feelings about the freedom of his country. He devoted his life's work to this cause. Although Muñoz Rivera did not get all that he wanted for Puerto Rico, he did play a big role in improving his country's situation. His fight for Puerto Rican rights is the subject of this chapter.

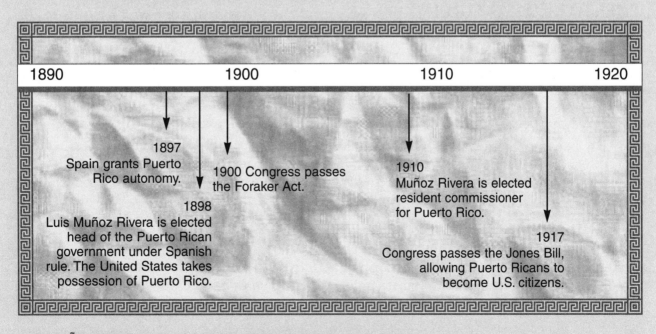

1890   1900   1910   1920

1897
Spain grants Puerto
Rico autonomy.

1900 Congress passes
the Foraker Act.

1898
Luis Muñoz Rivera is elected
head of the Puerto Rican
government under Spanish
rule. The United States takes
possession of Puerto Rico.

1910
Muñoz Rivera is elected
resident commissioner
for Puerto Rico.

1917
Congress passes the Jones Bill,
allowing Puerto Ricans to
become U.S. citizens.

The ancient Greeks had a myth about a king named Sisyphus (SISS-uh-fuss). The god Zeus (ZOOSE) was angry at Sisyphus and punished him. After Sisyphus died, he had to push a huge rock up a mountain again and again until the end of time. Whenever Sisyphus got almost to the top, the rock rolled back down the mountain. Without a rest, Sisyphus started his task anew.

When the United States took Puerto Rico, Luis Muñoz Rivera (LOO-ees MOON-yose ree-VAIR-uh) thought of Sisyphus. Muñoz Rivera was a Puerto Rican political leader and poet. He and others had worked for years to persuade Spain to let Puerto Ricans govern themselves. Finally Spain agreed. In 1898, Muñoz Rivera had become the head of an elected Puerto Rican government.

This experiment with autonomy had barely started—and then it was over. The United States took Puerto Rico from Spain. Then it sent its own people to run the island. Like Sisyphus, Muñoz Rivera had to start again at the bottom of the hill.

SECTION 1:
PUERTO RICO IS A COLONY OF SPAIN.

Muñoz Rivera devoted his life to the goals of liberty and freedom. He struggled, through his politics and his poems, to improve life for the Puerto Rican people. He became a hero to later generations.

Uprising Against the Spanish Muñoz Rivera was born at a time of change in Puerto Rico. Almost four centuries had passed since Christopher Columbus claimed the island and its gold in the name of Spanish kings. Spanish

Writer and political leader, Luis Muñoz Rivera devoted his life to the goals of Puerto Rican liberty and freedom.

colonists had carved out settlements on the island. They had tried to enslave the 30,000 or more Arawak people who lived there. Within a century, war and disease had wiped out the Arawaks. Then the Spanish brought enslaved Africans to work in Puerto Rico's sugar fields.

When Muñoz Rivera was born in 1859, slavery still existed in Puerto Rico—as it did in the South of the United States. The Civil War put an end to U.S. slavery by 1865. In Puerto Rico, slavery lasted until 1873.

In 1868, a brief uprising against Spanish rule took place at the small Puerto Rican town of Lares (LAH-res). The revolt is known as *el Grito de Lares* ("the Outcry at Lares"). Within three days, Spanish soldiers had crushed it.

Setbacks for the Liberals The following year, Spain allowed Puerto Ricans to elect representatives to the Spanish parliament. Puerto Ricans could elect town governments.

The right to vote was tightly restricted. In the first place, only men could vote. Second, voters had to know how to read and write. Five out of six men could not read or write, so they could not vote. Finally, voters had to own property and pay taxes. Thus, only a small minority qualified to vote.

Events in Spain and the Caribbean soon put an end to most of Puerto Rico's freedoms. Harsh new rulers took over in Spain. They wanted to crush a rebellion that had broken out in Cuba. They also wanted to re-establish firm control over both Puerto Rico and Cuba. In 1875, they sent Puerto Rico a new governor. He dismissed liberal mayors and closed Puerto Rico's legislature.

Storekeeper, Poet, or Activist? In Muñoz Rivera's family, politics was a subject of hot debate. Muñoz Rivera's father was a conservative. His uncle was a liberal. Muñoz Rivera listened to their endless talks about politics. He formed his own ideas at an early age.

Muñoz Rivera had to decide what he was going to do with his life. His father was an important man in a small town in the central mountains. The elder Muñoz was a landowner and merchant. For a time he was the town's mayor.

Young Muñoz Rivera went into business as a storekeeper. However, his real interest was politics. He began to write about politics for newspapers and magazines. He also continued to write poetry.

Muñoz Rivera became the leader of his town's Liberal party. At a party convention, he read one of his poems. It was about hope and faith and struggling for a better future. The audience cheered him for his inspiring words.

The Push for Self-Rule By 1887, the Liberals felt that the time was right to call for autonomy for Puerto Rico. They gave their party a new name: the Autonomist party. They stressed that they were not asking for independence from Spain—only for self-rule.

Puerto Rico's governor did all he could to stop the Autonomist party. The governor imposed military rule. He had 400 Autonomists thrown in jail. Some of the prisoners were beaten or tortured.

Finally the government in Spain heard what was happening. It fired Puerto Rico's governor and had the prisoners released. But Spain showed no desire to grant the island autonomy.

Making a Deal The Autonomists decided that the best way to reach their goal of self-rule was to make an alliance with a political party in Spain.

In 1896, Puerto Rico's Autonomists sent Muñoz Rivera and three others to Spain to work out a deal. On his own, Muñoz Rivera made an arrangement to support the Spanish Monarchist party if they would grant autonomy to Puerto Rico.

Autonomy At Last The agreement worked. When the Monarchists took power, Puerto Rico received a Charter of Autonomy from Spain.

Under the new Charter, Puerto Ricans elected their own legislature and town governments. Most decisions about Puerto Rico were to be made by Puerto Ricans.

Muñoz Rivera led a six-man Executive Council that took office immediately. Puerto Rico's new legislature met for the first time on July 18, 1898. But the timing was very bad. One week later, U.S. troops landed on the island.

The U.S. takeover of Puerto Rico was swift and complete. Within hours, U.S. troops had entered the armory of the Spanish and seized control of all arms and ammunition.

The Cuban-Spanish-American War As you have read, war had broken out between Spain and the United States in April 1898. In just a few weeks, the United States seized the Philippines and Cuba. Then, on July 25, 1898, U.S. troops landed in Puerto Rico. Within a few days, it controlled the island.

Thinking It Over

1. How was Puerto Ricans' right to vote restricted by Spain?

2. What long-term goal did Muñoz Rivera accomplish in 1897?

SECTION 2:
PUERTO RICO DEALS WITH A NEW COLONIAL MASTER.

The United States took over Puerto Rico from Spain. For a time, Muñoz Rivera remained in office. But relations between Americans and Puerto Ricans got off to a bad start.

The Americans wanted to run things their own way. They looked on the Puerto Ricans as children who needed adult supervision. General Guy V. Henry, the U.S. military governor, wrote a friend:

> I am getting in touch with the people and trying to educate them to the idea that they must help govern themselves, giving them kindergarten instruction in controlling themselves without allowing them too much liberty.

Tough Words Muñoz Rivera had many quarrels with General Henry. It did not help that neither man spoke the other's language. Muñoz Rivera knew only Spanish. General Henry knew only English. They had to depend on an interpreter.

Once, in a fit of anger, General Henry told the interpreter, "Tell Muñoz I'm sick of hearing him argue about every decision I make. So far I haven't lost my temper, but I've knocked down bigger men than him."

Muñoz Rivera had a quick reply. "Please inform the general that if he undertakes to behave violently toward me, I will be obliged to throw him out of the window."

Within a few months, Muñoz Rivera resigned. But he did not give up the battle for Puerto Rican self-rule. Like Sisyphus, he would start over at the beginning.

Back to Square One The United States considered Puerto Rico a valuable military base. From Puerto Rico, U.S. ships could guard the sea lanes to Central America.

Congress passed laws to keep Puerto Rico under strict U.S. control. The **Foraker Act** of 1900 laid down the new rules. The act ended military rule in Puerto Rico and put U.S. civilians in charge. Officials in Washington, D.C., appointed the governor and the heads of major departments.

The Foraker Act gave Puerto Ricans only a shadow of their former rights. They had a legislature, and could elect the lower house. But Americans appointed the upper house. Under its autonomy charter from Spain, Puerto Rico had elected its own representatives to the Spanish parliament. The representatives had full voting rights there. Under the Foraker Act, Puerto Ricans elected a single representative to the U.S. Congress. This person, called a **resident commissioner,** could take part in congressional debates but had no vote.

Low Standard of Living Spanish rule had done little to develop the economy of Puerto Rico. The island had almost no industries. Most farmers scraped a bare living from the land. Many people had no land of their own. A few months a year they might do the back-breaking work of cutting sugar on large plantations. The rest of the year they went hungry.

Moreover, diseases were a constant threat. There were few doctors. Sewers and other sanitation measures were inadequate. Education for most people was very limited. Only one school-age child in twelve had a chance to go to school. A small layer of educated people had studied at Spanish universities. Puerto Rico itself had no university.

Still, Puerto Rico had a vibrant culture made up of the diverse people who lived there. Roughly half of the people were of Spanish descent. One fourth were of African descent. The other one fourth were a mixture of Spanish and African.

Early Measures U.S. rule brought improved sanitation and new public health measures. People began to live longer.

Land was very scarce in Puerto Rico. The island's 930,000 people were crowded into an area about half the size of Connecticut. Much of the land was mountainous, so it was not suited to crops.

The Foraker Act put a limit of 500 acres on the amount of land one person or company could own. But that rule was ignored. Four large U.S. sugar companies and a U.S. tobacco company bought up land. They created vast plantations. Before long, they were the dominant forces in Puerto Rico's economy.

Continuing the Fight Muñoz Rivera kept up his fight to win autonomy for Puerto Rico. In 1901, he moved his family to New York. There he started a newspaper called the *Puerto Rico Herald*. Part of the newspaper was in Spanish and part in English. This newspaper helped the small Puerto Rican community in New York keep up the fight for self rule.

Before long, Muñoz Rivera was back in Puerto Rico, deeply involved in politics.

Many Puerto Ricans fought well for the United States in Europe during World War I. Here, in 1919, after the war was over, a Puerto Rican platoon parades through the streets of San Juan.

Like many Puerto Rican leaders, Muñoz Rivera wanted the United States to admit Puerto Rico as a state. But that seemed a long-range goal. First, he worked to get the Foraker Act changed.

Representing Puerto Rico In 1910, Muñoz Rivera was elected resident commissioner. He went to Washington to take up his non-voting seat in the House of Representatives. He decided he would have to learn English if he expected to do any good. It wasn't easy, but in a year or so he was able to get along comfortably in English.

For six years, Muñoz Rivera represented Puerto Rico in Congress. He met with the President. He testified before committees. He worked to get a better deal for Puerto Ricans. It was a hard and lonely job. Muñoz Rivera wrote to a friend:

I am here alone, in a tomb-like isolation. I mix with people who speak a different tongue, who have no sympathy for my way of life. They are not even hostile but indifferent, cold, and rough as the granite stones which support their big Capitol.

El Bill Jones In 1916 a member of Congress introduced a bill to change the terms of the Foraker Act. For the first time, the bill would make Puerto Ricans U.S. citizens. They would also gain new political rights. Puerto Ricans called this legislation *El Bill Jones* ("the Jones bill"), after the man who introduced it.

In Muñoz Rivera's eyes, the bill had many flaws. It gave Puerto Rico much less autonomy than it had had under the Spanish. He worked hard to get improvements written into the bill. In a moving speech, he asked the United States to give Puerto Ricans more rights as a step toward full independence. Thus, he said, the United States could show that it was truly "a great liberator of oppressed peoples."

In the end, however, Muñoz Rivera had to accept what was offered. Sick and unhappy, he returned to Puerto Rico while the bill was still before Congress. In November 1916, he died.

The Jones Bill passed Congress in March 1917. Under its terms, Puerto Rico's governor, judges, and top cabinet officials were still appointed from Washington. But Puerto Ricans could now elect both houses of their legislature. As U.S. citizens, they

In 1952, Puerto Rico became a commonwealth. For the first time, the flags of Puerto Rico and the U.S. flew together over San Juan.

Congress to give Puerto Rico full autonomy. He was Puerto Rico's first elected governor, serving four terms from 1949 to 1965.

In 1952, Puerto Rico became a **commonwealth,** in free association with the United States. Commonwealth is a status unique to Puerto Rico. The island's residents are U.S. citizens. Trade moves freely between the island and the mainland. Puerto Ricans are eligible for benefits under U.S. law. However, they pay no federal income tax. On the other hand, their resident commissioner still has no vote in Congress. And Puerto Ricans cannot vote in presidential elections.

The issue of statehood is still a hotly-debated topic. In 1993, Puerto Rico held a referendum. Of those who voted, 48 percent wanted to keep the status of commonwealth. Another 46 percent favored statehood. And 4 percent backed independence.

could move to the mainland and come and go as they pleased. They could also be drafted into the U.S. army. Many Puerto Rican men fought for the United States when the country entered World War I later in 1917.

Another Muñoz Muñoz Rivera's son, Luis Muñoz Marín (mah-REEN), carried on the fight for greater autonomy. From the 1930s to the 1960s, he led a powerful movement for change. "Operation Bootstrap," started under his leadership, gave Puerto Rico's economy a sharp boost. Later, Muñoz Marín persuaded

The Muñoz Legacy In the end, Muñoz Rivera attained many, but not all, of the goals for which he struggled. He left a legacy on which future generations of Puerto Ricans could build.

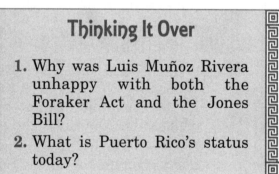

Thinking It Over

1. Why was Luis Muñoz Rivera unhappy with both the Foraker Act and the Jones Bill?

2. What is Puerto Rico's status today?

CHAPTER 16 REVIEW

I. REVIEWING VOCABULARY

Match each word on the left with the correct definition on the right.

1. autonomy
2. resident commissioner
3. commonwealth

   a. title given to Puerto Rico's representative in Congress

   b. self rule

   c. a self-governing nation with political and economic ties to another country

II. UNDERSTANDING THE CHAPTER

1. What was *el Grito de Lares*?
2. What were the terms of Puerto Rico's Charter of Autonomy from Spain?
3. What political changes did the Cuban-Spanish-American War bring to Puerto Rico?
4. Why was Puerto Rico valuable to the United States?
5. What did the Jones Bill give Puerto Rico?

III. APPLYING YOUR SKILLS

1. **Reading for the Main Idea** Reread the subsection on page 145 titled "The Push for Self-Rule." Write one sentence that expresses the main idea of each paragraph in the subsection.
2. **Drawing Conclusions** Reread the beginning of Section 2. From the statements of General Henry, what conclusions can you draw about the attitude of the Americans toward the Puerto Ricans?

IV. WRITING ABOUT HISTORY

1. **What Would You Have Done?** Imagine that you lived in Puerto Rico in 1898 when the United States took over the island. Write an editorial for a Puerto Rican newspaper expressing how you feel about the takeover and what action you think the people of the country should take.
2. **Past to Present** Write a magazine article that discusses how Puerto Rico today compares with the Puerto Rico of Muñoz Rivera's last years.

V. WORKING TOGETHER

Form a group with several classmates. Together, create a poster showing a timeline of Puerto Ricans' struggle for autonomy, with illustrations of significant events.

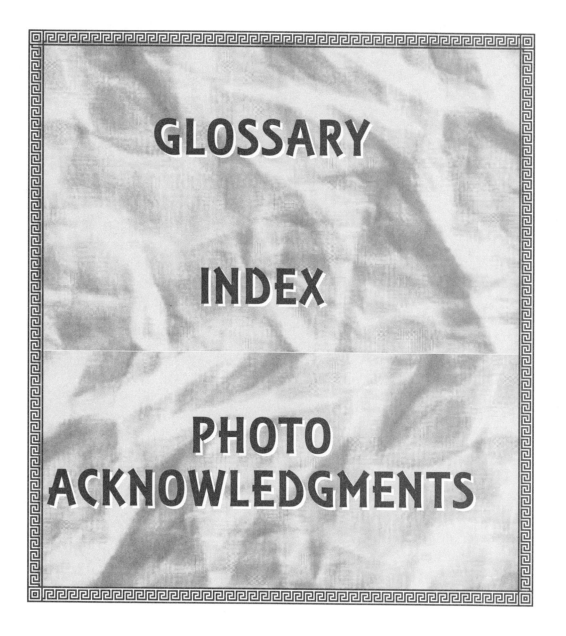

GLOSSARY

INDEX

PHOTO ACKNOWLEDGMENTS

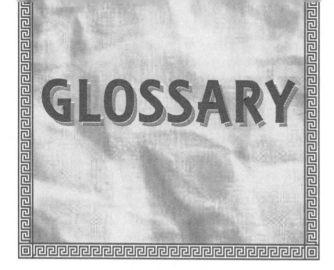

GLOSSARY

abolition a movement that called for an end to slavery (58)

annex to add onto a territory or nation (91)

autonomy self-rule (143)

blockade to close off an area, usually by troops or ships (44)

border states slave states that remained in the Union (118)

cadet a young military student (90)

causeway a raised road over a lake (12)

cavalry a branch of the military made up of soldiers that fight on horseback (20)

civil service all government jobs, except for elected positions or those in the military (109)

commonwealth a self-governing nation with strong political and economic ties to another nation (149)

contraband property of one country that an enemy has the right to seize during a war; used during the Civil War to describe a runaway African American slave behind Union lines whom the North refused to return to a southern owner (119)

democracy a form of government in which citizens rule either directly or indirectly (6)

dialect a regional language (128)

emancipation the freeing of slaves (120)

expansionism a policy under which one country expands its borders by taking over the land of another country (91)

fong an organization made up of Chinese families who banded together to help each other (103)

freedmen freed slaves (130)

Gullah a dialect spoken by African Americans on the Sea Islands, South Carolina; a blend of West African languages with an old form of English (128)

hypocrisy (hih-POC-ruh-see) pretending to be concerned about something one really does not care about at all (52)

imperialism a policy by which one country takes control of other countries or regions (137)

industrialization the process of developing factories, railroads and other forms of industry (66)

inherit to receive something when a relative dies (73)

kindergarten a pre-school for young children (77)

Koran the Muslim holy book (20)

lobby to try to influence public officials (82)

Loyalists colonists who supported the British during the American Revolution (53)

manifest destiny the U.S. goal of expanding its borders from the Atlantic to the Pacific oceans in the 1800s (91)

mission a settlement whose chief purpose is to convert people to the Christian religion (27)

missionary a priest or a religious person who works to convert people to the Christian religion (28)

multicultural of many cultures (7)

negotiate to meet with others to settle a dispute (84)

neutral supporting neither side in a disagreement, war, or other conflict (44)

nomad a person who moves from place to place in search of food (28)

normal school a teacher's college (66)

Patriots colonists who fought for independence from Britain during the American Revolution (42)

petition a written request to the government or to someone in charge (57)

prejudice an unfair opinion about someone or something (35)

presidio a fort (28)

rancho (RAHN-choh) a farm where cattle are raised (47)

ransom payment that is demanded to free prisoners (21)

reform to change something for the better (74)

resident commissioner a representative to the U.S. Congress from Puerto Rico that could take part in debates but has no vote (147)

scapegoat a person or group of people that has been wrongly blamed (34)

secede to withdraw officially from a country or organization (76)

seminary a private school that provides specialized instruction (63)

slave codes laws designed to limit the activities of African American slaves (24)

synagogue a Jewish house of worship (35)

taboo (tah-BOO) something that is forbidden; a prohibition (136)

tenant farmer a farmer who rents land from a landowner and pays the rent with a portion of the crops he or she grows (100)

transcontinental extending or going across a continent (98)

tribute a tax or payment that conquered people pay to their conquerors (11)

urbanization the movement of increased numbers of people into cities, or urban areas (67)

vaquero (vah-KEH-roh) a cowhand (47)

veteran a person with experience, especially in the military (112)

yuen a cooperative farming company organized by Chinese immigrants (103)

INDEX

PHOTO ACKNOWLEDGMENTS

7: (top left) The Granger Collection; (top right) Culver Pictures Inc.; (center) The Bettmann Archive; (bottom right) The Bettmann Archive; (bottom left) The Virginia Historical Society; **9:** (top left) The Postcards and Stereocard Collections. Centro de Estudios Puertorriquenos, Hunter College, CUNY; (top right) Hawaii State Archives; (center) California Historical Society, San Francisco. Photographer A. D. Marchand FN=23451; (bottom right) Brown Brothers; (bottom left) Brown Brothers; **10:** The Bettmann Archive; **12:** Scala/Art Resource, N.Y.; **13:** Copyright British Museum; **16:** Stock Montage Inc.; **18:** Mercury Archives/The Image Bank; **20:** The Granger Collection, New York; **21:** Mercury Archives/The Image Bank; **22:** Brown Brothers; **26:** Courtesy Museum of New Mexico, Neg. 149798; **28:** Stock Montage Inc.; **29:** Print Collection Miriam and Ira D. Wallach Division of Art, Prints and Photographs, The New York Public Library Astor, Lenox and Tilden Foundations; **30:** National Museum of American Art, Washington/ Art Resource, N.Y.; **34:** Stock Montage Inc.; **36:** The New York Historical Society; **37:** American Jewish Historical Society; **38:** American Jewish Historical Society; **40:** American Jewish Historical Society; **42 and cover:** Florida State Archives; **44 and cover:** Florida State Archives; **45:** The Louisiana Collection, State Library of Louisiana; Baton Rouge, Louisiana; **48:** Florida State Archives; **50:** The Bettmann Archive; **52:** Chicago Historical Society; **54:** The New York Historical Society; **56:** The Virginia Historical Society; **57 and cover:** Massachusetts Historical Society; **58 and cover:** Mercury Archives/The Image Bank; **59:** Culver Pictures, Inc.; **62:** Nebraska State Historical Society, Soloman D. Butcher Collection; **64:** The Bettmann Archive; **67:** The Bettmann Archive; **69:** The Bettmann Archive; **70:** Atlanta University Archive; **72:** Mary Evans Picture Library; **74:** Culver Pictures, Inc.; **75:** The Granger Collection, New York; **76:** The Bettmann Archive; **78:** Culver Pictures, Inc.; **80:** The Bettmann Archive; **82 and cover:** Western History Collection, University of Oklahoma; **84 and cover:** The Granger Collection, New York; **88:** Mary Evans Picture Library; **90:** Stock Montage Inc.; **91:** Mercury Archives/The Image Bank; **92:** Stock Montage Inc.; **94:** D. Donne Bryant; **96:** The Bettmann Archive; **98:** Denver Public Library, Western History Department; **100:** California Historical Society, San Francisco. Photographer A.D. Marchand FN-23451; **101:** The Bettmann Archive; **102:** The Bettmann Archive; **106:** Culver Pictures, Inc.; **108:** Massachusetts Commandery Military Order of the Loyal Legion and the U.S. Army Military History Institute; **110:** Brown Brothers; **111:** Brown Brothers; **113:** Brown Brothers; **116:** Collection of The New York Historical Society; **118:** Brown Brothers; **119:** Brown Brothers; **120:** Mercury Archives/The Image Bank; **121:** The Granger Collection **122:** Brown Brothers; **126:** The Granger Collection; **129:** The Bettmann Archive; **131:** Brown Brothers; **132:** Culver Pictures Inc.; **134:** Hawaii State Archives; **136:** Hawaii State Archives; **138:** Brown Brothers; **142:** Harper's Weekly; Centro de Estudios Puertorriqueños, Hunter College, CUNY; **144:** Centro de Estudios Puertorriqueños, Hunter College, CUNY; **146:** Harper's Weekly; Centro de Estudios Puertorriqueños, Hunter College, CUNY; **148:** UPI/Bettmann; **149:** UPI/Bettmann.